Jacob
I Have Loved

Jacob
I Have Loved

Lance Lambert

Sovereign World

Sovereign World Ltd
PO Box 784
Ellel
Lancaster LA1 9DA
England

Unless otherwise stated, all Scripture quotations are taken from the American
Standard Version, with "Jehovah" changed to "the LORD" by the author.
Copyright © 1901 (public domain); mg = margin note.

Other versions used are:
KJV – King James Version. Crown copyright
NKJV – New King James Version. Copyright © 1982 by Thomas Nelson, Inc.
Used by permission. All rights reserved.
NASB – New American Standard Bible. Copyright © 1960, 1962, 1963, 1968,
1971, 1972, 1973, 1975, 1977, 1995 by The Lockman Foundation. Used by
permission.
JND – John Nelson Darby Version. Public domain.
LB – The Living Bible. Copyright © 1971 Tyndale House Publishers.

ISBN: 978 1 85240 476 5

The publishers aim to produce books which will help to extend and build up
the Kingdom of God. We do not necessarily agree with every view expressed
by the authors, or with every interpretation of Scripture expressed. We expect
readers to make their own judgment in the light of their understanding of
God's Word and in an attitude of Christian love and fellowship.

Cover design by David Lund Design
Typeset by CRB Associates, Reepham, Norfolk
Printed in Malta

CONTENTS

Dedicated to Alan and Marjorie Redpath.
From them I learned the first lessons
in discipleship and devotion to the Lord,
both through teaching and example.
I will be forever thankful to them.

Foreword

The title of this book compresses into four tiny words a mystery that has puzzled and confused, daunted and deterred many people and many nations over many centuries! *How on earth, and why on earth, can God love "Jacob"?*

While the Old Testament draws to a close with an affirmation of this truth out of the mouth of God (Mal. 1:2), the Epistle to the Romans, majoring on New Testament doctrine, builds a whole chapter around the theme (Rom. 9: see esp. v. 13)! Mystery though it may be, this same declaration of God's elective love has also proved to be of indescribable encouragement to many.

Coming as I do myself from a long line of "Jacobs," I can commend this book to you totally without reservation. It is far, far more than a mere overview of a fascinating Bible story. It is far, far more than a mere portrayal of important biblical events. Rather, this is a vibrant example and a living portrayal of how the Lord plans and waits to minister into the lives of us all – including your life and mine.

I cannot overemphasize this fact – I do not believe that there is any character in the Bible, other than the Lord Himself, from whom we can learn such hard lessons, and yet gain such great encouragement. In these increasingly difficult days – days of lukewarmness in the faith everywhere in the West, of superficiality in the teaching of the Word of God – it is such a stimulant to find "meat" of the Word to eat, instead of "milk" to drink. The Church, the Body of Christ, can benefit so much from what the Lord has given to Lance to share in these pages.

Little in our lives today is more important and more needed than personal spiritual growth. For those concerned about "preparation" – "Make ye ready the way of the Lord, Make his paths straight..." (Matt. 3:3b) – I am convinced that Lance Lambert's discernment (and humor) in this account of God's dealings with Jacob are worth 1,000 sermons. Of all his books and Bible teachings, I regard this as the apex, the spearhead, the most important of all else that Lance has shared in his worldwide teaching ministry. I have personally benefited from it in my three earlier readings of the forerunner of this final issue.

Jacob *is* a mystery: *How* can God possibly love him? *Why* does God seem to stand aside while he deceives his own father, Isaac, allowing Isaac to summon him – *"Come closer!"* – before pronouncing that intractable blessing over him, thinking he was blessing Esau? *Why* does God permit this? *Why* does God bring blessing into your life and mine – can we honestly say, "Because we deserve it!"?

Why does God stand aside while Jacob himself is deceived into marrying Leah – something he does not discover until the next morning!? *Why?* There are no slick answers to such questions. But Lance unfolds the sovereignty of God as operative in Jacob's life – inevitably leading him into not only God's purposes, but into a transformation of his inner nature.

The plain fact is that, whether we admit it or not, like it or not, we are all Jacobs at heart! What a statement this is to make! The name "Jacob" carries with it such shame, such depravity, that few of us relish even the thought, let alone the reality, of being tarred with such a name and nature. But, again, *whether we like it or not*, our Bible – the "Manufacturer's Instruction Manual" – tells us:

The heart is deceitful above all things, and it is exceedingly corrupt...

(Jer. 17:9)

When we look at the Hebrew root of the word translated "deceitful," we find that the scripture could easily be rendered as "The heart is 'jacob'd' and desperately sick." The root word (meaning "supplanter") from which Rebecca and Isaac named Jacob, is the same word used to describe our human hearts!

Jacob's "disease," his inner nature (if you will), is something that has come to us all from Adam. It is not merely a Jacob phenomenon. It is something we are all born with, as Scripture tells us, and, in His grace, the Lord grants us a lifetime during which He works to bring us back to a resemblance of Himself.

In other words, while Jacob is the progenitor of the twelve tribes (why on earth did God choose him!?), he is also precisely the model from which God wants us to discern what we ourselves are like, or are capable of. Well, what an "artist" Lance is – because (for me at least) he paints an infallibly accurate picture in this book. It is true that this book may pummel you (that will do you good); it is true that it may dismay or distress you (God will lift you up); but without doubt you will end up with a clearer mind and a higher resolve to become the person God intends you to be: the overcomer, the one who contends with, and who – because of his self-life – struggles with God but prevails!

As you may know, Jacob was not without tears in his battles. Such tears can wash away evil, can show the Lord we are serious about the desire to be changed. *The victory, the reconciliation with Esau, the transformation in Jacob, all came without effort **after** his all-night struggle and his being alone with God.*

Our great God specifically selected and elected a vessel as imperfect as Jacob to follow Abraham and Isaac in fathering the nation God was going to use to bring the Word of God, the Lamb of God and the Spirit of God into this world.

> Who hath known the mind of the Lord? or who hath been his
> counsellor? . . . For of him, and through him, and unto him, are
> all things. To him be the glory for ever. Amen.
>
> (Rom. 11:34, 36)

In the same way, the Lord has chosen you (and me!), with all
our foibles and weaknesses. He has plans for you that are
beyond your wildest dreams. In the Hebrew "Art Gallery" of
Hebrews chapter 11, the last picture we have of dear Jacob, that
former cheat, arch-deceiver, and twister, is the glorious one of
him worshiping God, leaning on the top of his staff (totally
dependent upon God) and *blessing* (Heb. 11:21).

How God, the great and mighty Potter, who loved Jacob,
and who loves you and loves me – how He waits and yearns to
continue and to complete in us all that reshaping, that work of
His hands, that only a divine skill and a divine love could
conceive and accomplish. Even Jacob will be in that bridal
procession! This is something that comes out of the heavens
above through the work of no one less than the Holy Spirit –
quite beyond our human wisdom.

May the revelation and inspiration behind the writing of this
book be factors in truly bringing you also into the relationship
with the Lord that Jacob knew after his struggle at Jabbok. God
had been preparing Jacob for that time for twenty-one years.
And has He not been preparing you also? Jacob's "strength" lay
in his cry to the Lord: "I will not let thee go, except thou bless
me" (Gen. 32:26)!

May that same cry be sincerely yours as you read on.

Ken Burnett

Chapter 1

DUST AND GLORY

In the beginning of the Bible God states in the simplest of words that "the LORD God formed man of the dust of the ground, and breathed into his nostrils the breath of life; and man became a living soul" (Gen. 2:7 KJV). In that one statement the whole constitution of man is explained. Years later, Abraham speaking of himself said,

> Behold now, I have taken upon me to speak unto the Lord, who am but dust and ashes...
>
> (Gen. 18:27)

In one of his best-loved psalms, King David wrote,

> For he knoweth our frame;
> He remembereth that we are dust.
> As for man, his days are as grass;
> As a flower of the field, so he flourisheth.
> For the wind passeth over it, and it is gone;
> And the place thereof shall know it no more.
>
> (Ps. 103:14–16)

When man fell he contradicted a fundamental and essential principle in his creation. Although he was made from dust, yet

into that dust God had breathed spirit, and man had become a
living soul. God had breathed something of Himself into man.
Consequently, man's makeup is threefold: spirit, soul, and body
(see 1 Thess. 5:23; Heb. 4:12). The soul of man differs from the
soul of animals, or birds, or fish, in that it has this eternal
element.

Therefore man can never be satisfied with the dust that he is,
nor even with the mere life of his soul. Without God, man is
dust. He is "of the earth," "earthy." Mere flesh, with all its
energy, its creativity, even its genius, can never satisfy him. In
the book of Ecclesiastes the Preacher, with profound simplicity,
declares,

> He hath made everything beautiful in its time: also he hath set
> eternity in their heart, yet so that man cannot find out the
> work that God hath done from the beginning even to the end.
>
> (3:11)

We should note the phrase "he hath set eternity in their heart."
Hence, in the heart of every lost human being, in his or her
spirit, there is an "eternal vacuum." That vacuum can only be
filled with the God of glory. With anything less, man can never
be satisfied. The fact is that when he fell, man lost the very
meaning of his existence. In poignant words the Lord describes
that condition,

> in the sweat of thy face shalt thou eat bread, till thou return
> unto the ground; for out of it wast thou taken: for dust thou
> art, and unto dust shalt thou return.
>
> (Gen. 3:19)

David states, in the psalm that I have already quoted, that
the Lord knows our frame and remembers that we are dust,
and declares that as a good human father has compassion and
feeling for his children, so the Lord pities those that fear Him.

He describes the condition of man as frail and transient; indeed as fragile as the flowers of the field, "here today and gone tomorrow." Then, by the Spirit of God, David says,

> But the lovingkindness of the LORD is from everlasting to everlasting upon them that fear him ...
>
> (Ps. 103:17)

For those who are in a saving and covenant relationship with God, our "dust" is encompassed from eternity to eternity by the lovingkindness, the grace and mercy of the Lord. It is a deeply moving revelation. David uses the Hebrew word *hesed*, translated in the quotation above as "lovingkindness." It is a word that cannot be translated by one English word. The Revised Version, American Standard Version, J.N. Darby Version, and New American Standard Bible translate it as "lovingkindness"; the King James Version and New King James Version translate it as "mercy"; Revised Standard Version as "steadfast love"; New International Version as "love." This Hebrew word is used 246 times in the Old Testament. It speaks of the undying, persevering, steadfast, merciful, loyal, covenant love of God for those who belong to Him. In the Hebrew New Testament the Greek word for "grace," *charis*, is often translated *hesed*. So strong and great is God's grace that David declares in the same psalm:

> For as the heavens are high above the earth,
> So great is his lovingkindness towards them that fear him.
>
> (v. 11)

In other words, this "steadfast love," this grace of His, is immeasurable. It is immensely powerful and strong.

In our frail, worthless, and transient dust, there is something eternal; but in our unsaved condition, it is empty and dead. When the Eternal God enters our spirit through the saving work of the Lord Jesus, we are made spiritually alive. That "eternity" God has placed within the heart, which I have described as an "eternal vacuum," is now indwelt and filled by the Lord. A new day has dawned for us, with a new life and a new power. In the end, even the dust out of which our bodies were formed, will be brought to glory! For the salvation won for us by Christ Jesus is so full and complete that it includes not only the redemption of our spirit and our soul, but even the redemption of our physical body.

If ever a man was dust, a vessel of clay, it was Jacob. No other character in the Bible more clearly illustrates this. His flesh was gifted, intelligent, shrewd, discerning, and, at times, cunning and deceitful. He was truly of the earth, earthy. Yet, no other biblical personality has had greater influence upon all that followed him than Jacob. From one point of view, Abraham was the historic turning point in the history of redemption. He is, after all, "the father of all who believe." Yet the redeemed of the Lord are not called Abraham, or Isaac, or Moses but they are called Jacob.

God calls Himself specifically the God of Jacob twenty-one times (e.g. 2 Sam. 23:1; Ps. 20:1; 46:7; 75:9; 81:1; 84:8; Isa. 2:3; Mic. 4:2). The name of Jacob is eternally linked with the name of God, with the eternal purpose of God, and forever entwined with the people of God. Again, we discover that when God speaks of His relationship to Jacob, He speaks of Himself as Jacob's Savior and Redeemer, the Mighty One of Jacob (e.g. Gen. 49:24; Ps. 132:2, 5; Isa. 49:26; 60:16). Redemption is one of the great themes of the Bible. Literally it signifies the recovery of property or persons by a kinsman; the liberation or release made effective by the payment of a ransom; or the payment of a required price to secure the release of a convicted criminal. When we understand the meaning of redemption, we have come to the heart of the matter concerning Jacob.

The central fact of Jacob's story is that the Lord Himself was his redeemer. The story of Jacob is *the* illustration of that which

God can do with any life He redeems. He redeems us from captivity to the powers of darkness and evil; from the power of sin; from bondage to the temporal and to vanity. He redeems us from an empty uselessness into a living union with Himself. We are rescued and restored to the original purpose, and, through His work of redemption, called to His eternal glory. The apostle Peter states this simply:

> And the God of all grace, who called you unto his eternal glory in Christ, after that ye have suffered a little while, shall himself perfect, establish, strengthen you.
>
> (1 Pet. 5:10)

This is Jacob's story.

Amy Carmichael expressed all this truth in an extraordinary poem that she wrote, which came out of her own deep experience of the Lord. She entitled it "Dust and Flame."

> But I have seen a fiery flame
> Take to his pure and burning heart
> Mere dust of earth, to it impart
> His virtue, till that dust became
> Transparent loveliness of flame.
>
> O Fire of God, Thou fervent Flame,
> Thy dust of earth in Thee would fall,
> And so be lost beyond recall –
> Transformed by Thee, its very name
> Forgotten in Thine own, O Flame.

The amazing truth is that Jacob's name has not been lost in the debris of human history, nor has it been forgotten, as have so many other names. Incredibly, it is forever linked with God. His story is an integral part of the history of divine redemption. Only the Lord Himself could bring a Jacob to such a position. Only He could bring a Jacob to His glory.

The powerful work of God through the Holy Spirit was to transform Jacob into Israel: to make the redeeming work of God a reality in him. In one place the Lord, speaking of the people of God as Jacob, says,

> For I, the Lord thy God, will hold thy right hand, saying unto thee, Fear not; I will help thee. Fear not, thou worm Jacob, and ye men of Israel; I will help thee, saith the Lord, and thy redeemer is the Holy One of Israel.
>
> (Isa. 41:13–14)

The Lord takes something as worthless and as insignificant as dust, and makes it material for eternal glory and beauty. He takes someone as earth-bound as a worm and, by His Spirit, places within the heart, within the spirit of that redeemed person, a divine homing instinct. Such a one will end in the throne of God and in the glory of God.

It takes many of us who are children of God, redeemed by His grace, a lifetime to come to the simple recognition that we are dust, with all the earthbound, earth-imprisoned qualities of dust. Nevertheless, once the God of all grace takes hold of us, once He redeems us, we discover that in the Messiah we are called to His eternal glory, and nothing less. This is Jacob's story. It is also our story. The Lord will never rest until He has brought us to such glory. He will do the same work He did in Jacob, with the same power and determination, and the same boundless grace and mercy in every other Jacob whom He redeems.

Chapter 2

JACOB I HAVE LOVED

[T]hat the purpose of God according to election might stand, not of works, but of him that calleth, it was said unto her, The elder shall serve the younger. Even as it is written, Jacob I loved, but Esau I hated … and that he [God] might make known the riches of his glory upon vessels of mercy, which he afore prepared unto glory, even us, whom he also called …

(Rom. 9:11b–13, 23–24a)

… the glory of Jacob whom He loveth.

(Ps. 47:4 mg)

On a number of occasions in the Word of God, the Lord declares His love for Jacob. The little phrase "Jacob I have loved" is perhaps one of the most wonderful and remarkable words that God ever spoke. Those who have little knowledge of their Bible and no knowledge of the story of Jacob – his history and character – would not be taken back by this statement: "I loved Jacob." On the other hand, if you know something about Jacob, then these words are radiant with the beauty of God's grace, of His mercy and love. They contain great encouragement for all those who know their own heart and nature. The fact that it is repeated in the Bible more than once, means that it has real significance. Furthermore, it is linked to a theme in the Bible, which, though not very popular today, is nevertheless one of its greatest themes: Divine Election.

Jacob the loved one

Preachers sometimes declare that the Old Testament ends with a curse. Technically they take the very last words of the book of Malachi in English, which says, "lest I come and smite the earth with a curse." This is a very strange way of reading the book. I do not think that the message of Malachi ends with a curse at all. In my estimation, it is a profound declaration of God's undying love for His people.

We find this declaration in the words at the very beginning of the book,

> I have loved you, saith the LORD. Yet ye say, Wherein hast thou loved us? Was not Esau Jacob's brother? saith the LORD: yet I loved Jacob; but Esau I hated...
>
> (1:2–3)

Just as remarkable is the word in Malachi 3:6: "For I, the LORD, change not..." – and you would think that He would go on to say, "Therefore, beware, for judgment will fall on your unfaithfulness and fickleness!" Instead, He says,

> For I, the LORD, change not; therefore ye, O sons of Jacob, are not consumed.

In other words, the power of God, the infinity of God, and the love of God are thrown on the side of His redeemed people, weak and sinful though they are. How wonderful is such a revelation! The invincible strength and the sovereign authority of God are for the weak "Jacobs" He redeems. The writer of the Hebrew letter, by the Spirit of God, puts it this way,

Wherein God, being minded to show more abundantly unto the heirs of the promise the immutability of his counsel, interposed with an oath; that by two immutable things, in which it is impossible for God to lie, we may have a strong encouragement, who have fled for refuge to lay hold of the hope set before us ...

(6:17–18)

There is no character in the Bible, except, of course, the Lord Jesus, by which the whole people of God have been named. I have already made mention of this. The names "Jacob" and "Israel" have been given to the people of God forever. We discover, as we read our Bible, that both the prophets and the psalmists speak of the redeemed as a corporate Jacob and a corporate Israel.

The New Testament makes it clear that those of Gentile background, who have been saved, are no longer alienated from the commonwealth of Israel.

Wherefore remember, that once ye, the Gentiles in the flesh, who are called Uncircumcision by that which is called Circumcision, in the flesh, made by hands; that ye were at that time separate from Messiah, alienated from the common-wealth of Israel, and strangers from the covenants of the promise, having no hope and without God in the world. But now in Messiah Jesus ye that once were far off are made nigh in the blood of Messiah.

(Eph. 2:11–13)

And again,

that the Gentiles are fellow-heirs, and fellow-members of the body, and fellow-partakers of the promise in Messiah Jesus through the gospel.

(Eph. 3:6)

By the grace of God such have been grafted into that olive tree which is the Israel of God. How amazing these statements are!

The name of *Israel*, which we normally understand as a people, as a nation, and then as the redeemed of the Lord, actually began with one man called *Jacob*. The Lord did something in his life and changed him into *Israel*. From then onwards both the name *Jacob* and the name *Israel* were given to the people of God. It seems therefore that there is something of vital importance and significance to learn about the man Jacob.

The first and fundamental lesson we learn is that the love of God for Jacob is the key to everything in his history and life. So often we consider the love of God to be a Sunday-school theme, a "kindergarten" subject. We are so familiar with it that we could easily lose its real import. The love of God is not sentimental or "sugary"! It is powerful and determined; one could even describe it as passionate and fearful in its range. How tremendous are these wonderful words, "Jacob I have loved." They explain everything.

Jacob the twister

I would not want to do any disservice to Jacob, or demean or devalue him, because one day I will meet him. Therefore I want to be careful in the manner in which I write about him. Jacob was not, as is so often understood, an ugly, mean, unattractive character, a swindler of swindlers, full of deceit and cunning, with every dark and evil thing nestling in his heart. That kind of man is the typical picture which the anti-Semite paints of the Jew. It is not a true picture of Jacob. For one thing Jacob must have been a highly intelligent and attractive man, because we find in the scriptural record some quite remarkable inferences.

All the three women in his life, his mother, Rebecca, and his two wives, Leah and Rachel, apparently found him very attract-ive! Rebecca must have felt there was something very appealing about Jacob. From the manner in which Rebecca acted, it would seem that she had some deep intuitive feeling that Jacob had the character to inherit the birthright and the blessing, and not Esau. Was it only the prophetic word which she received before the twins were born that caused her to go to such lengths for Jacob?

Then again, it seems to me that Rachel was attracted to Jacob from the moment she first saw him. The fact that he kissed her after he rolled back the stone on the well, so that her sheep could be watered, is remarkable. In the Middle East setting, then and now, it would be unthinkable! That Rachel was neither confounded nor repelled by his kiss speaks volumes (see Gen. 29:10–11).

It is the same with Leah. It is apparent that she desired Jacob as much as Rachel. What was his appeal since he was penniless at the time? Neither Rachel nor Leah were marrying into riches, so into what were they marrying? There must have been something unusually appealing and attractive about Jacob. It is apparent to me that Leah willingly fell in with Laban's strategy to marry her to Jacob, knowing full well that Rachel had been promised to him, and that he would marry her in the end. If he was the spineless, anemic, round-shouldered, home-loving man that he is so often depicted, one wonders what it was that so attracted both of Laban's daughters.

The Scripture, in fact, describes Jacob as a "home-loving man" (see Gen. 25:27). Interestingly the word used in Hebrew, *tom*, can be translated "perfect," "complete," "sound," or "wholesome"; and even has a meaning of complete or healthy physical strength. It is an interesting fact that when Jacob came to the region in which Laban lived, he found a whole number of flocks waiting to be watered. From the story, it emerges that the circular stone covering the well was a large and heavy one, and needed a number of shepherds to move it. The fact that Jacob single-handedly moved the stone for Rachel, reveals that he was no weakling (see Gen. 29:1–12). Furthermore the fact that he wrestled all night with the Heavenly Visitor is further evidence that Jacob was no wimp (see Gen. 32:24–26)!

The difference between Jacob and Esau is often portrayed as the difference between an open-air type, athletic and physically strong, and a home-loving type, non-athletic and physic- ally weak. This picture does not match the reality. Apart from the other evidence, the fact that Jacob was a shepherd contra- dicts the picture so often painted of him. There is no doubt that Esau was an athletic open-air type, the kind of man who was as happy to sleep outside the home as in it. Yet as a shepherd, Jacob must have had qualities of endurance and rugged- ness. He must have slept many times outside with his flocks, although as a choice he preferred to sleep under his own roof.

The meaning of Jacob's name

Over against this portrayal of Jacob we have to recognize the meaning of his name. When Jacob was born, he was born the second of twins. His mother Rebecca had had a rough and difficult time with them in her pregnancy, and had asked the Lord for the meaning of it. The Lord told her,

> Two nations are in thy womb, And two peoples shall be separ- ated from thy bowels. And the one people shall be stronger than the other people. And the elder shall serve the younger.
>
> (Gen. 25:22–23)

Of course, it was not a question of who was truly the elder, because these two boys were born at the same time. The situation of normal brothers, who would be born with at least a year between them, does not hold in the event of twins. Twins are born on the same day and normally at the same hour. In this instance, Esau was born first, and Jacob was born with his arm twisted around Esau's heel. In the light of that which the Lord had said to Rebecca, this was held to be highly significant by the family. In Hebrew the word "heel" is *aqeb*, and the word "supplant" or "twist" is *aqab*. Thus they named him "Jacob" (Gen. 25:26). *Ya'aqob* is a play on the word "heel," "twist," and "supplant." The meaning of his name was that he took hold of his brother's heel as if he would pull him back and be born first. Literally, his name meant "heel-grabber" or "heel-holder." It can best be understood as "twister" or "supplanter." The idea was that by stealth or shrewdness he intended to displace his brother and supplant him. At his birth the traits that were to become more and more apparent with the progress of time, were revealed. It is interesting to note Esau's words,

> Is not he rightly named Jacob? for he hath supplanted me these two times. He took away my birthright. And, behold, now he hath taken away my blessing.
>
> (Gen. 27:36)

Jacob, true to his name!

There can be little discussion about the fact that Jacob was a brilliant businessman. He had shrewd business acumen. It was within his nature not only to sense a good deal but also to clinch it. He was by nature acquisitive. He was the type of person who always prospers and who always makes money. In whatever condition or situation Jacob found himself, he always profited by it.

It is instructive that when the story is read clearly and objectively, it becomes evident that Jacob did not *want* to deceive. In fact, when his mother planned the strategy for obtaining the blessing and revealed it to Jacob, he said, "My father will surely say that I am a deceiver when he hears the voice of Jacob and feels my arms and neck and finds that I am smooth skinned and not hairy like my brother Esau." It is also interesting to note how scandalized Jacob was about the cheating and swindling of his Uncle Laban. It is in a highly indignant manner that he said to his wife Rachel,

> your father has deceived me, and changed my wages ten times;
> but God suffered him not to hurt me.
>
> (Gen. 31:7)

This reveals that Jacob did not realize or recognize his own nature and its strength. In other words, the problem with Jacob was not that he was some unattractive sharp-dealer from the underworld, but rather that he had a nature which he was unable to control. His nature *controlled him* and he was unaware of it.

The strength of Jacob's nature

There is an unlovely side to Jacob, which may often have been hidden. Nevertheless, it was there. It only needed the right circumstances and pressures to be brought out into the open. When his twin brother came in from an unsuccessful day of hunting, faint and hungry, he smelt the food Jacob was cooking and asked for a portion. Jacob saw his opportunity to obtain the birthright of the firstborn and immediately went for it. "You can have as much as you want, if you will only sell me your birthright." Apparently Jacob was a good cook!

The Word of God describes Esau as a despiser of his birthright. He had little time for the things of God and of eternity. On the other hand, whatever faults Jacob may have had, he valued the things of God. For him the birthright and the blessing had real significance. Deep down within Jacob's heart there was a recognition of divine things and their value. He wanted to obtain them because he realized that those were the things that truly mattered. What he could not control was his own natural strength and energy. He could not wait for God to work; he had to work in order to obtain them.

I imagine Jacob must have known of the prophecy that was given to his parents before his birth. His mother, who adored him, must surely at some point have spoken to him about it. Without doubt, early on in his life he understood that the Lord had a very especial purpose for him. He recognized that the birthright and the blessing would be important elements in it. How the Lord would have brought both of these to him, we do not know. What we do know is that Jacob himself worked it, obtaining them by very questionable means.

If the way he stole his brother's birthright was questionable, the incredible lengths to which he went to steal the blessing is shocking. It was his mother who planned the deception of his nearly blind father in order to obtain Esau's blessing, the blessing of the firstborn. The fact that she planned it, however, is no excuse for Jacob. Jacob only questioned his mother's plan for fear that his father would detect his deception of him. Nonetheless, he fully cooperated with her in its implementation. Jacob had no answer to the strength of his own nature. It swept him along.

When he went to his Uncle Laban, God promised that He would increase his flocks and prosper him, but Jacob had "to help" the Lord. He adopted a stratagem which involved seeking to influence the pigmentation of his and Laban's flocks by visual stimuli. By this technique he increased his flocks to the detriment of Laban's flocks.[1] Jacob clearly knew that God had specifically promised to prosper his flocks but he could not leave the matter with the Lord. He had to help Him. The Lord could have fulfilled His promise without Jacob's questionable help!

Jacob's problem is also our problem

We have thousands of Christians who see something of the Lord but then try to "get the whole operation off the ground."

1. The *Encyclopedia Judaica* has a very interesting article on this matter under the heading of "biology."

The mess that follows is incredible. Many of us will surely recognize what happens when we, newly saved, barge into the family and try to convert them all at "gunshot," until the family is sick to death of us. The fact of the matter is that we have understood what is right and we wish to be faithful. Nevertheless, instead of it being the Lord working *through* us, we are working *for* the Lord. There is a profound difference between working *for* the Lord and working *with* the Lord.

Then again, consider the thousands of believers who see the truth of the house of God, the Church, and then try to set it up. The Church scene is littered with tragedies because people believe they have seen what is the Church and then tried to put it into operation. We have apostles who are not apostles; prophets who are not prophets; elders who are not elders; deacons who are not deacons; ministers who are not ministers; and we have churches that are not the Church expressed. We have people who are supposed to be authorities sent by God, and God never sent them. We use scriptural terms and set up systems; we build hierarchies; we create whole routines; we institutionalize the organic; we substitute natural techniques for the work of the Holy Spirit. Left to ourselves we make such a mess of the Church!

What is the basic problem? It is not that our heart does not want the Lord; our heart does want the Lord. Our problem is the strength of our natural life. We cannot control it. As soon as we see the value of the birthright, we are going to clinch the deal and obtain it, always, of course, "with God's help." When we see the value of the blessing, we will obtain that blessing even if there has to be a little deception in it. Nevertheless, we will not rest until we have obtained it. Our attitude is that it will not "drop out of heaven on us." If mother has to work her tricks by sowing up calf and goatskins, and Jacob has to sound gruff like his twin brother Esau, it is the end that justifies the means. Even if before Jacob was born, God has promised that the elder would serve the younger, He has to be helped for His word to be fulfilled. We have "to use our common sense"!

Jacob met his match when he met Uncle Laban. The two of them tried to outwit each other for twenty years. It was the Lord's way to bring Jacob to a recognition of himself. He worked seven years for Rachel and ended up with Leah. It was Uncle Laban's work! Jacob was scandalized that his own uncle would do something like that. Seven years is not a short time and there are probably few husbands who would work seven years to obtain their wives, and that without any salary! Imagine the shock if you had worked seven years for the one you had set your heart upon, and did not receive her, but received instead her sister. The trouble is that we make the scriptural story sound so beautiful, when the reality was different. The Lord used this to bring Jacob to an end of his own natural strength, and to bring him to the place of desperation, to the place where God could meet him and transform him. In Laban he saw his own twistedness.

God's irrational love

In spite of all Jacob's failings, his weaknesses, even his sin, the words of the Lord echo through the corridors of time, "Jacob I have loved." The love of God cannot be explained! Why did the Lord so love Jacob? Some will say, "Well, of course, God saw something in Jacob that was beautiful; that is why He loved him." I am not sure that this is the explanation. Consider the way the Lord speaks about this matter. For example, in Deuteronomy:

> For thou art a holy people unto the Lord thy God: The Lord thy God hath chosen thee to be a people for his own possession, above all peoples that are upon the face of the earth. The Lord did not set his love upon you, nor choose you, because ye were more in number than any people;

for ye were the fewest of all peoples: but because the LORD
loveth you . . .

(7:6–8a)

And again:

Behold, unto the LORD thy God belongeth heaven and the
heaven of heavens, the earth, with all that is therein. Only
the LORD had a delight in thy fathers to love them, and he
chose their seed after them, even you above all peoples, as at
this day.

(10:14–15)

This statement of the Lord is remarkable for its simplicity and
straightness. The Lord was declaring that He set His love on
them because He loves them. The Lord set His love on Jacob
because He loved him. There is no other real explanation. Why
does the Lord love you? It is a good question! One might be able
to find some features about you as to why God loves you. I can
only state that I find myself at a total loss as to why God loves
me! It is beyond my understanding and I can only come back to
this word, "The Lord loves you because He loves you."

Do not question why certain people fall in love with one
another, although it is a normal and natural event. Sometimes
you meet a person who loves somebody else so passionately
and completely that you are left wondering what on earth he or
she sees in that one! For that person, however, the one he
or she loves is the most beautiful creature that ever graced this
earth, and everything about them is lovable. Such love is
beyond understanding; it is inexplicable and incredible. You
cannot place it under a microscope to examine its makeup, or
analyze its components.

Sometimes we like to think that God loves us because He has
plans to use us, but is that the explanation of His love for us?
When you come to a place where you fail, then the devil will

come to you and say, "Your Lord does not love you anymore for you have lost your usefulness to Him; your value to Him is lost." It is as if we believe that the Lord is some kind of shrewd mastermind with a high business acumen, who weighs the pros and cons about us, and considers how best He could exploit us for His own purposes. This is not true. It is a lie! In some incredible manner that is far beyond our understanding God loves us because He loves us. He loves you because He loves you, and that is the heart of this whole matter. That is why the names of *Jacob* and *Israel* are given to the redeemed people of God. There can be no other explanation for the persevering and steadfast love of God for Jacob; it is beyond reason and is, in one sense, irrational. We could describe it as the irrationality of divine love.

The wonder of God's love

The wonder of God's love is tremendous. He did not say, as He could have well said, "Israel I have loved." If He had said that, theologically one could understand it: He loved Israel because Israel was the converted, the changed, and the transformed Jacob; Israel was the perfected Jacob. God would rather forget the old Jacob; He only ever really loved Israel. However, we have no record, concerning Jacob the individual, that God ever said, "Israel I have loved," although, of course, it would be true. He said, "Jacob I have loved." In other words, He takes the lowest denominator; He takes the person at his worst and says, "I love him." "I chose him because I love him."

Chapter 3

Vessels of Mercy Afore Prepared

The apostle Paul, by the Spirit of God, declares,

> [T]hat the purpose of God according to election might stand, not of works, but of him that calleth, it was said unto her, The elder shall serve the younger. Even as it is written, Jacob I loved, but Esau I hated ... and that he [God] might make known the riches of his glory upon vessels of mercy, which he afore prepared unto glory, even us, whom he also called...
>
> (Rom. 9:11b–13, 23–24a)

This statement is strangely foreign to the contemporary ear. We are so democratic in our whole concept of thought that we have to wrestle with such ideas. In fact, we can only be satisfied if we are able to explain them away. It is difficult for us to understand why God said, "Esau I have hated," although the idiom in the original Hebrew is not as harsh as it sounds in translation. Nevertheless, we think that it is an unfair and unjust severity; and although we would not express it in words, we consider such an attitude to be wrong. The divine statement, "vessels that he endured with much long-suffering, vessels of wrath fitted for destruction" (see Rom. 9:22), seems so strange to our modern mentality. Nonetheless, it is the Word of God.

However, the positive side is glorious: "vessels of mercy afore prepared unto glory." My salvation did not begin with a decision I made. It reaches back into prehistory eternity, that period which the Bible describes as "before times eternal." Someone answers, "Surely you understand that God in His foreknowledge saw your decision for Him and chose you based on your choice." It seems strange that He chose you only because you chose Him! Is not the very obvious meaning of "choice," or "to choose," devalued by such an idea? Consider these words: "that God might make known the riches of His glory upon vessels of mercy afore prepared unto glory." Is this preparation explained by God's foreknowledge? In other words, did He prepare everything about our background, our circumstances, our relationships, and our genetic history that would make us "vessels of mercy"? What you are declaring is that the Lord chose you and loves you because you chose Him. In my estimation that is an untenable view.

God loves you because He loves you!

It is a cause of great thankfulness to God if you came to a point where you made a decision, or signed a decision card, or put your hand up, or went forward, or knelt at some penitent stool. Whatever you did, thank God He brought you to that point. Nevertheless, there is a prehistory to your decision, and that prehistory is this: "Jacob I have loved." God loves you because He loves you and not because you chose Him.

Think of those wonderful words in John 15, "Ye did not choose me, but I chose you, and appointed you, that ye should go and bear fruit" (v. 16a). What mysterious words! What a universe of meaning beyond the ability of our finite minds to comprehend. It is not open to question that we have a serious responsibility to exercise our will, but beyond and above that we discover the mystery of election. Our finite mind will never be able to understand it, but we worship God for it.

We have a statement of our Lord Jesus recorded in John 6 which has never been satisfactorily explained by those who emphasize *only* the free will of man:

> Jesus said unto them. I am the bread of life: he that cometh to me shall not hunger, and he that believeth on me shall never thirst. But I said unto you, that ye have seen me, and ye believe not. All that which the Father giveth me shall come unto me; and him that cometh to me I will in no wise cast out. For I am come down from heaven, not to do mine own will, but the will of him that sent me.
>
> (vv. 35–38)

Carefully note the conjunction "For" at the beginning of verse 38. It links the earlier statements which the Lord Jesus made in verses 35–37 with that which follows.

All that which the Father hath given Me

What did the Lord Jesus mean by the phrase "the will of him that sent me"? It is clear that it is the will of God that those whom the Father has given to the Son should come to Him and should experience the salvation of God through the Lord Jesus. This becomes even clearer in the sentence that follows:

> And this is the will of him that sent me, that of all that which he hath given me I should lose nothing, but should raise it up at the last day.
>
> (v. 39)

This is a wonderful declaration! I had no idea until I first began to see this matter that my salvation has a prehistory, that it reaches into "before times eternal," and on to "the eternal ages to come." "All that which the Father giveth me shall come unto me." Somewhere in that pre-time eternity, the Father said to the Son that you would be one of those He was giving to Him, and you came to Him. It matters not how you came; it was certainly through the work of the Lord Jesus. The Father has given you to the Son. If the Lord tarries, and we die and are buried, at the last day, as the Lord says, He will raise us up with a new body, a redemption body, a resurrection body. What a salvation! The only possible explanation for this is that He has set His love on you.

Where does it all begin and where does it all end? It begins with God and it ends with God. Our problem is how we come into it. Some assert that one must be very careful of this kind of doctrine and teaching, and I agree. There are people who have taken this truth to such an extent that they will not preach the gospel to the unsaved, they will not even have children's work, or a Sunday school, or distribute any Christian literature, or lift a finger to help in evangelism, because they say it is God's sole prerogative to save. It is certainly clear that when our Lord gave the command to the disciples, it was to go into *all* the world and preach the gospel (see Mark 16:15). We have no right to countermand this. How can the unsaved hear and how can the great purpose of God be fulfilled unless there are those who hear the Lord's command and obey?

Opposite ends of the same truth!

The Word of God clearly states this:

> Whosoever shall call upon the name of the Lord shall be saved. How then shall they call on him in whom they have not believed? and how shall they believe in him whom they have not heard? and how shall they hear without a preacher? and how shall they preach, except they shall be sent? even as it is written, How beautiful are the feet of them that bring glad tidings of good things! ... So belief cometh of hearing and hearing by the word of Christ.
>
> (Rom. 10:13–15, 17)

We should note that these words are found in connection with predestination and election. So whilst we have, on the one hand, man's responsibility before God to exercise his own free will, on the other hand, this is balanced perfectly with God's prerogative in election. These two matters are opposite ends of the same truth, and are too much for our finite minds to comprehend or hold together. As far as we are concerned, we have a responsibility to shoulder and fulfill: to reach the lost, to preach the gospel, to be faithful in our witness. Yet we must always remember that only God can save a human being. It is good for us to remember the comment made by that great preacher of the gospel and servant of the Lord Charles Haddon Spurgeon that in the pulpit he preached for all to be saved, but on his knees he believed only the elect would respond.

The apostle Paul, a chosen vessel

How is it possible to explain the conversion of the apostle Paul? There he was with a certificate in his pocket, on his way full of fire and zeal to destroy the believers, and suddenly about midday, somewhere on the Golan Heights on the road to Damascus, the Lord appeared to him and struck him to the ground. This rabbi, Saul of Tarsus, called out, "Who are You, Lord?" And the Lord said, "I am Jesus whom you are persecuting." I do not read of any decision being made or any card being signed or any hand being raised. Something happened to the man. How is it to be explained? I cannot explain it, but I do know that which the Lord said to Ananias about Saul: "Go thy way: for he is a chosen vessel unto me" (Acts 9:15).

It is often stated that somewhere or other the apostle must have been challenged or had an argument within himself. Paul stated, in fact, that the Lord had questioned him: "Why do you kick against the goads?" What were those goads? Maybe one of them began when he saw Stephen being stoned. Or other goads could have been the brutal way he dealt with believers before his conversion, and the manner in which they had responded. Nevertheless, none of this is recorded in the Word of God. When one reads Paul's testimony, given at various points in Acts and in his letters, he speaks of his conversion as a sovereign act of God. It is certainly true that he must have responded when the Lord said, "I am Jesus." He could have refused Him out of hand, and thus rejected Him.

Years ago I knew an old man who was the father of two sons, both of whom became well known in the work of God in Britain. He told me how he was converted. He was a captain in the Merchant Navy. He was a man who liked to drink and often used to get drunk. By his own confession, he was a "bad lad." In such a state he would go home, wreck things in the home, and even treat his wife roughly. One night he went home in a drunken stupor, forced his way through the front door, fell flat on his face, rolled over on his back, and stayed in that posture on the drawing-room floor for the whole night. He came round the next morning with a hangover, thoroughly converted. The first thing he said to his wife when he got up off the floor was, "Have we a Bible in this place?" She thought he must still be suffering from drink and said to him, "Are you going to make fun of even the Bible?" However, he was not drunk, he was converted. He said to me, "I did not even want the Lord. Sometimes at sea I thought about God, and I thought about my sins, but I did not want God, yet God took hold of me." His wife then chimed in and said, "Do you know how I found the Lord? Two weeks later, I was sweeping the corridor (in those days they did not have vacuum cleaners), and I stopped for a moment and lent on the broom. I was so amazed at the change that had come over my husband and thought to myself, 'What on earth has happened to him?' And there, leaning on the broom, I was converted."

Of course, most of us have had a different experience: somewhere we have heard the gospel and made a response. I myself was saved through reading the story of C.T. Studd. It was the first Christian book I ever read. I was nearly thirteen years of age. The next day, when Alan Redpath issued an appeal in the Sunday evening service, I stood up. It was the second Christian service I had ever been in. If anyone had asked me anything about Christian doctrine or the Bible I could not have answered. All that I can say is that God saved me. It is wonderful, however, to hear the other side of the coin, and to know that even when we have made a decision for the Lord and responded to Him, that is not where the history of our salvation began. It reaches back into eternity, into the heart of God where He set His love upon us. Do not ask me to explain the many complex questions that arise out of this. I only know that this man Jacob, whose name was given to the redeemed people of God forever after, was a vessel of mercy *afore prepared* unto glory.

Consider, then, the strength and determination of the love of God. To be loved by God is at one and the same time both the most glorious thing in the universe and the most fearful thing. So often in our Christian circles this whole matter of love has become sentimental. We think of God as some dear, old, white-haired gentleman with whom you could get away with anything. It is that idea of love which has robbed us of a genuine understanding of His love. To be loved by God is both the most wonderful thing and the most fearful thing in the universe.

The gifts and calling of God are irrevocable

For example, take the words of the apostle Paul in Romans 11:29, "For the gifts and the calling of God are irrevocable." Their first and primary connection is to the Jewish people, although the statement is generally taken as having connection only to the church or to Christian servants of God or to Christian missions. If, however, one reads the previous verses it becomes clear that the primary relation is to the Jewish people:

> As touching the gospel, they [the Jews] are enemies for your sake: but as touching the election, they are beloved for the fathers' sake. For the gifts and the calling of God are not repented of [irrevocable].
>
> (Rom. 11:28–29; cf. NASB)

What do I mean that it is both a wonderful thing and a fearful thing to be loved by God? If I take the story of the Jewish people I see an outstanding illustration of this truth. God has never forsaken the Jewish people, throughout the course of time, because of His love for them. To this very day, He has persevered because of that steadfast love. He has followed them through all their alienation and divorce from Him, through the massacres, persecution and hatred of them, through the cruelty of the Crusaders and of the inquisition, through the pogroms and the holocaust, to the recreation of the state of Israel and its eight wars. In all the bloodiness of the last two thousand years of Jewish history, He has been present, He who dearly loves them. He has never let them go and will not let them go until finally He has won them. Stage by stage, little by little, He will shut them up, cornering them until they are utterly alone, without anything or anyone to lean on. Then the alternatives will be stark: they will face either total destruction or the Lord. He will not rest until they fall into His arms. Such is the wonder and the fearfulness of the love of God.

To be loved by God: both wonderful and fearful

On the one hand, there is nothing more wonderful than to be loved by God, to experience the tenderness, the mercy, and the abounding grace in His love. Every true child of God can testify to His love expressed in the way He leads us and sometimes follows us; the way He endures our rebellion. Indeed, He never leaves us nor forsakes us, even though we make a mess of our lives. To know that our sins have been blotted out as a thick cloud, removed as far as the east is from the west, cancelled by the grace of God, is to experience His love. Only that love and grace of God could have justified us in His sight and declared us to be righteous through the finished work of Christ.

On the other hand, it is also the most fearful thing to be loved by God. For once He loves you, He will wait a whole lifetime until finally He has won you fully. Even on a deathbed He will bring His loved one to a place where they will yield on an issue. I have known a number of such people. They should have yielded on those issues long before; but they would neither yield nor surrender until finally, in the weakness of death, they said, "Lord, I surrender."

Never for a moment think that your circumstances, the difficult relationships in your life, the impossible situations, the seemingly insoluble problems, are haphazard. They are not, for God is behind them. They are divinely arranged. It may not be apparent at the time but it is His love in action. To be a vessel of mercy afore prepared unto glory is a matter full of awe.

God corners Jacob

How did the Lord deal with Jacob? It seems to me that in this man so loved by God we see the abounding grace of God in such clear colors. Jacob had an incurable natural strength about him, a nature that could not be suppressed. In fact, the more he tried to suppress it, the more irrepressible it proved to be. God knew that and remembered the dust that Jacob was; He knew Jacob's "frame." If God had challenged Jacob and sought to break him from the beginning, with one pulverizing blow sought to transform him, it would have failed. Jacob would neither have listened, nor would he have cooperated. Indeed, he would have rebelled with all his strength. Instead, the Lord allowed him to steal both the birthright and the blessing, causing him to flee from the home he loved so much. For twenty years he lived away from his home. He never saw his beloved mother again, with whom he had such a close relationship. It is worth noting that when she had produced the strategy for Jacob to steal the blessing, and Jacob protested, she had said, "Let your curse be on me . . ." (Gen. 27:13 NKJV). It did indeed fall on her; for the rest of her life she never saw her Jacob again. Nevertheless, behind all of this, mysteriously, stood the God of love.

It was the same with the twenty years that Jacob spent with Laban. He met his match in Laban, because Laban was another "Jacob." The two outwitted each other for all of those years until, in the end, desperate, Jacob finally learned the lesson and the Lord could say to him, "Return unto the land of thy fathers and to thy kindred; and I will be with thee;" and Jacob obeyed and returned. In all of this we see how God marvelously arranged these circumstances. Through abject fear of his twin brother Esau, at that point coming to meet him, he was left alone. Then, and only then, did the mysterious Visitor appear. Jacob had been thoroughly prepared for the greatest encounter of his life. He wrestled all night with that One, because deep within Jacob there was a witness that this was his time. It was the love of God. It had taken all of those years for the Lord to corner his beloved Jacob, but He won the battle. When the Lord said, "What is your name?" Jacob said, "Jacob." It may not seem to be so apparent but in actual fact Jacob was "owning up" to being Jacob. "It shall no longer be Jacob but Israel," said the Lord. It was as if the Lord was saying, "Jacob, finally I have you."

To me this is incredibly comforting and encouraging! Maybe what I have written may frighten some, but if you really value the things of God, if you make eternal matters the priority in your life, you will find this message of tremendous encouragement. I know only that one of my greatest fears has been that somewhere along the line I might let go of the Lord. Then I think to myself, "There will be no reward, no city, no throne; little glory, many tears, only barely saved." It is in that moment that the words from the heart of the Lord come back to me, "Jacob I have loved." The solid fact is that *He* will not let me go! To know that God, having loved me and chosen me that His purpose according to election might stand, will follow me throughout my life, using my circumstances, my situations, and my problems to fulfill His work in me, is of tremendous encouragement.

We must never forget that the Lord has a goal in view. With that aim in mind He will use our background, our tempera-ment, and even our genetic history. All will be employed by Him to change us into the likeness of His Son. The Lord will use the relationships in our families, our relationships at work and in business, our relationships in church-life and in the work of God. He will not fail.

From Jacob to Israel

> But now thus saith the LORD that created thee, O Jacob, and he that formed thee, O Israel: Fear not, for I have redeemed thee; I have called thee by thy name, thou art mine. When thou passeth through the waters, I will be with thee; and through the rivers, they shall not overflow thee: when thou walkest through the fire, thou shalt not be burned, neither shall the flame kindle upon thee. For I am the LORD thy God, and Holy One of Israel, thy Saviour . . .
>
> (Isa. 43:1–3a)

How amazing are these words! The Lord declares that He created Jacob and Israel He formed, and that in all the work required to transform us from Jacob to Israel, we are not to fear; His redeeming grace and mercy will be the key. Such a work will require us to pass through waters and through rivers, to walk through fire, but He promises to be with us.

"They shall not overflow thee." Is that not a description of situations or circumstances which seem to threaten our very existence by drowning us? Yet the Lord's redeeming love is there: you will pass *through* them. Or again, "thou shalt not be burned, neither shall the flame kindle upon thee." You will not be burnt up by the problems or the circumstances, for in the fire you will discover Him. In fact, the Lord will use these experiences, sometimes seemingly diabolical in nature, to work His work in you.

The apostle Paul described his experience of this graphically as a "thorn in the flesh," a "messenger of Satan" (see 2 Cor. 12:7–9). In a footnote on the Greek word translated "thorn" in Conybeare and Howson's *The Life and Epistles of St. Paul*, they state, "Stake is probably a more accurate translation." It would therefore seem to be more like the "agony of impalement" than the irritation of a thorn! Certainly it drove the apostle to experience the sufficiency of the Lord's redeeming grace so that he could testify that the power of God came to its full development in his weakness.

You will discover, as so many have, that God, not the devil, is behind these experiences. God is above them, beyond them, and using them. It is the love of God in action, albeit hidden! You will also discover that when such experiences come to us, it is all progress. You will pass *through* the waters, the rivers will not drown you; you will walk *through* the fire, the flames will not kindle upon you. If it were not the love of God, we would have much cause to fear, but it is the God of love.

Psychologists tell us that we all suffer from insecurity when we are not loved. If that is true, the Lord's people must be very insecure, lacking in their understanding and their experience of the love of God. Everywhere I travel I discover so many believers who feel insecure. They feel that there is a cloud in their relationship with God, as if God is angry with them; or that He has forsaken them, and failed them. Are you a Jacob? Maybe you think you are an Abraham, or an Isaac, or a Moses, or a Joshua. You may even think you are an Enoch. If you wish to think that, think it! The Lord has evidently a good deal more work to do in you. There are, however, some people who know that they are Jacobs. It is not that they are ugly, unintelligent, or unattractive; but there is a massive strength in their soul-life, a strength of self-will, an unbroken ego, and with it a zeal not according to true knowledge. You cannot break this condition yourself, for it is you! Here then comes a word of tremendous comfort. God loves you, and He loves you not because you are perfect, nor even because you are moving towards perfection, but He loves you because He loves you. He has chosen *you*. You are amongst His elect, born of His Spirit, and saved by His grace. His intention and determination is to change you from Jacob to Israel.

The jealous determination of God's love

Read some of the words of the Lord in the next chapter of Isaiah:

> Yet now hear, O Jacob my servant, and Israel, who I have chosen: Thus saith the LORD that made thee, and formed thee from the womb, who will help thee: Fear not, O Jacob my servant . . .
>
> (44:1–2b)

> Remember these things, O Jacob, and Israel; for thou art my servant: I have formed thee; thou art my servant: O Israel, thou shalt not be forgotten of me. I have blotted out, as a thick cloud, thy transgressions . . . the LORD hath redeemed Jacob, and will glorify himself in Israel.
>
> (44:21–22a, 23c)

It is the jealous determination of God that is *the* factor in Jacob's life. He seems so far from God in his character, in his attitudes, and in his ways. He was a bargainer, not a worshiper. Although the Lord repeatedly calls him "Jacob my servant," in truth he was not a servant of God. He was a manipulator of God, if that could be possible. Certainly, he was a manipulator of divine things. He saw the Lord as a means of prosperity, as a means of security, and as someone who was always there to lift him out of a mess. It was only when he became Israel that he loved the Lord for the same reason that the Lord loved him. He loved the Lord because he loved Him.

Only the grace of God could call Jacob, whether personally or corporately "My servant." The Lord fixes His eye on Israel, the one He will produce out of Jacob. It is altogether wonderful. He redeems Jacob, but it is Israel in whom He is glorified.

Do you love the Lord because you love Him? Or do you only love Him because He clears up the messes in your life, or because He provides you with some joy and exuberance, or because He creates for you some escapism from harsh realities? Do you love Him only because of what you obtain, or do you love Him for who He is? Would it not have been an appalling thing if the Lord had said, "I will have nothing to do with Jacob until he loves Me; I will not touch him whilst he has that bargaining spirit." The Lord, however, recognized all Jacob's weaknesses and, with a persistent and undying love, loved him from Jacob into Israel. That is what also He will do for you and for me. Such is the strength and determination of God's love.

What is the Church on earth if it is not a people who are being loved from Jacob into Israel? We are only too aware of the "Jacobs" in the Church. We can talk endlessly about the Church, its offices, its structure, its pattern, and much else; but unless we "Jacobs" are being transformed into "Israels," it is not a living Church. It is merely an historical institution, or an antique tradition, or a monument to past glory.

Jacob had many miles to travel in his spiritual pilgrimage. There were rivers that could not be avoided; through them he had to pass if he was to become Israel. There were fires through which he had to walk, trials he had to pass through, and difficulties with which he had to cope. It was, however, the God of love who had chosen him and, moreover, arranged the whole course of his life. God had arranged it so beautifully that the events which seemed most dark, even Satanic, were in truth employed by God to fulfill His purpose in Jacob's life.

If you know you are a "Jacob," the message of his life will be an enormous strength and comfort to you. For others, Jacob's life may not be so meaningful at present. They will only see his life as an object lesson. If, however, such children of God go on with the Lord, it will become a source of much encouragement. Jacob was a vessel of mercy afore prepared unto glory. So are we.

Chapter 4

THE PROMISED LAND

What was the purpose of God behind the election of Jacob? We know that God loved him; and there is no other reason for that love than that He loved him. What, however, was the goal of God's election? What did He have in mind for Jacob? God's purpose for Jacob was so vitally important, so significant in its scope, that He promised him: "I will not leave thee, until I have done that which I have spoken to thee of" (Gen. 28:15b). Since the whole redeemed people of God in time and eternity have been given corporately the name of Jacob and Israel, what can we learn from Jacob about our divine calling, both as believers and as the Church? We know from the words of the apostle Paul that "these things happened unto them by way of example, and they were written for our admonition, upon whom the ends of the ages are come" (1 Cor. 10:11). What then are the lessons we need to learn from Jacob?

The promised land: a land of covenant

> And, behold, the LORD stood above it, and said, I am the LORD, the God of Abraham thy father, and the God of Isaac. The land whereon thou liest, to thee will I give it, and to thy seed.
>
> (Gen. 28:13)

and the land which I gave unto Abraham and Isaac, to thee I
will give it, and to thy seed after thee will I give the land.

(Gen. 35:12)

The first lesson is to do with the land. It was a divinely given
and promised land. It was a land over which God Himself made
an unconditional covenant with Jacob's grandfather, Abraham,
and his seed after him:

And I will establish my covenant between me and thee and thy
seed after thee throughout their generations for an everlasting
covenant, to be a God unto thee and to thy seed after thee.
And I will give unto thee, and to thy seed after thee, the land of
thy sojournings, all the land of Canaan, for an everlasting
possession; and I will be their God.

(Gen. 17:7–8)

We should note that it is the Lord who establishes this
covenant, and it has no condition attached to it. It is made
through grace. We should also note that this covenant is
operative "throughout their generations." Twice the Lord uses
the word "everlasting" – firstly to do with the covenant and
secondly to do with the land. There has been much discussion
over the Hebrew word *olam*, translated "everlasting." If this
covenant was only for a certain time, it renders meaningless the
words "throughout their generations." It is clearly stated that
whilst there is a physical generation of the seed of Abraham
through Isaac, not Ishmael, and Jacob, not Esau, this covenant
is operative. If "everlasting" here means temporal, language
has lost its meaning. Again we need to note that the Lord
emphatically states two times that He will be their God,
whether that fact would be evidenced in blessing or in
judgment.

When we turn to Psalm 105 the psalmist, by the Spirit of
God, underlines this covenant:

> O ye seed of Abraham his servant, Ye children of Jacob, his
>   chosen ones.
> He is the LORD our God: His judgments are in all the earth.
> He hath remembered his covenant for ever,
> The word which he commanded to a thousand generations ...
>   (vv. 6–8)

A thousand generations stretches from the time of Abraham,
Isaac, and Jacob to far beyond our time. It is a further vivid
emphasis that this covenant is forever. The psalmist goes on
to say:

> The covenant which he made with Abraham, and his oath
>   unto Isaac,
> And confirmed the same unto Jacob for a statute, To Israel
>   for an everlasting covenant,
> Saying, Unto thee will I give the land of Canaan, The lot of
>   your inheritance;
> When they were but a few men in number, Yea, very few,
>   and sojourners in it.
>   (Ps. 105:9–12)

These statements are noteworthy!

Is that not marvelous? This was land that God covenanted to
give to Abraham, to Isaac, to Jacob, and to their seed after them.
As I have already underlined, this covenant was made with
Isaac and not with Ishmael, with Jacob and not with Esau. The
Lord, in fact, made a covenant with Ishmael, which He has kept
to this day (Gen. 16:7–13; 17:18–21; 21:18–21). It is of great
importance that we should remember that in the Messiah Jesus
God gives to the seed of Ishmael, and to the seed of Esau,
everything He gives to the rest of those who have tasted His
salvation. In the Lord Jesus there is no curse and no inequality;
the middle wall of partition has been abolished, and there is
only one new man. Nevertheless, the covenant concerning *the*

land was made not with the seed of Ishmael or of Esau, but with the seed of Isaac and of Jacob. It is operative to this day, since there is still a physical seed of Abraham alive on the earth.

We should note the fact that although the Lord made this covenant concerning the land with Abraham, Isaac, and Jacob, they never actually possessed the land. By faith they lived within it, believing that in the end the Lord would fulfill His promise and they would inherit it; and, in fact, their seed did inherit the land. They were an illustration of David's words in Psalm 37:3, "Trust in the LORD and do good; Dwell in the land, and feed on his faithfulness," or as the King James Version translates it, "And verily thou shalt be fed."

A land of provision

God clearly defined the boundaries of that land, and it is of vital importance to recognize that everything relating to the purpose of God was centered within it.

> Command the children of Israel, and say unto them, When ye come into the land of Canaan (this is the land that shall fall unto you for an inheritance, even the land of Canaan according to the borders thereof), then your south quarter shall be from the wilderness of Zin along by the side of Edom, and your south border shall be from the end of the Salt Sea eastward ... And for the western border, ye shall have the great sea ... And this shall be your north border: from the great sea ye shall mark out for you mount Hor ... And ye shall mark out your east border from Hazar-enan to Shepham ... This shall be your land according to the borders thereof round about.
>
> (Num. 34:2–12)

Everything they needed for national life, family life, business life, and spiritual life was there. The book of Deuteronomy describes that land:

For the LORD thy God bringeth thee into a good land, a land of brooks of water, of fountains and springs, flowing forth in valleys and hills; a land of wheat and barley, and vines and fig-trees and pomegranates; a land of olive-trees and honey; a land wherein thou shalt eat bread without scarceness, thou shalt not lack anything in it; a land whose stones are iron, and out of whose hills thou mayest dig copper. And thou shalt eat and be full and thou shalt bless the LORD thy God for the good land which he hath given thee.

(8:7–10)

Note carefully the words "thou shalt not lack anything in it." Whatever they needed was in that land.

A land in which the kingdom would be revealed

In that land alone the kingdom would come. It could not come in Babylon or Egypt or anywhere else. Within this land covenanted by God, the kingdom and the throne would be centered, representing the rule of God. David, the man after God's own heart, would be born and recognized in it, and would finally come to the kingdom and rule. The royal and Davidic line would be established within that land, from which the Messiah would spring.

Here the city of God would be built. In other words, Jerusalem would be possessed, to become the capital of that kingdom. This is the city of which alone of all the cities on the earth the Lord had said,

then it shall come to pass that to the place which the LORD your God shall choose, to cause his name to dwell there, thither shall ye bring all that I command you ... Take heed to thyself that thou offer not thy burnt-offerings in every place that thou seest; but in the place which the LORD shall choose ...

(Deut. 12:11, 13–14; cf. v. 5; Deut. 26:2)

Apart from any other consideration the phrase "the place which I choose to cause my Name to dwell there" is arresting and highly significant. Of no other city in the world did the Lord God so speak. The Lord took the city of Jerusalem to represent Himself, His mind and His heart, His character, His word, His purpose, His throne, His kingdom, and His salvation.

In no other city and in no other land could the house of God be built. The whole purpose of God was focused on the temple; all national life, family life, business life, and personal life was centered in it. The books of 1 and 2 Chronicles reveal to us that everything from the national to the personal, from the king to the individual, was judged by relationship to the house of God.

A land where the Messiah would come

Furthermore, in that land alone and in no other would the Messiah be born. Micah was to prophesy years later:

> But thou, Bethlehem Ephrathah, which art little to be among the thousands of Judah, out of thee shall one come forth unto me that is to be ruler in Israel; whose goings forth are from of old, from everlasting.
>
> (Mic. 5:2)

And Isaiah was to prophesy also:

> But there shall be no gloom to her that was in anguish. In the former time he brought into contempt the land of Zebulun and the land of Naphtali; but in the latter time hath he made it glorious, by the way of the sea, beyond the Jordan, Galilee of the nations. The people that walked in darkness have seen a great light: they that dwelt in the land of the shadow of death, upon them hath the light shined . . .
>
> For unto us a child is born, unto us a son is given; and the government shall be upon his shoulder: and his name shall be

called Wonderful, Counselor, Mighty God, Everlasting Father,
Prince of Peace. Of the increase of his government and of
peace there shall be no end, upon the throne of David, and
upon his kingdom, to establish it, and to uphold it with justice
and with righteousness from henceforth, even forever.

(Isa. 9:1–2, 6–7)

It is interesting to note that Isaiah predicted that the Messiah
would be associated with "Galilee of the nations" and with the
"way of the sea," called the "Via Maris," the ancient trade
route. It linked Egypt with Damascus and Babylon. The Lord
Jesus spent twenty-six years of His earthly life in a town a few
miles north of the Via Maris called Nazareth, and the three
years of His public messianic ministry in a town called
Capernaum, half a mile south of it. His life and ministry would
be forever linked to the Galilee. These prophecies of Micah and
Isaiah could not have been fulfilled anywhere else but in the
promised land.

Then again, in Malachi 3:1 it is prophesied:

Behold, I send my messenger, and he shall prepare the way
before me: and the Lord, whom ye seek, will suddenly come to
his temple; and the messenger of the covenant, whom ye
desire, behold, he cometh, saith the Lord of hosts.

The temple, the house of God, had to be rebuilt for this
prophecy to be fulfilled.

If Abraham, Isaac, and Jacob had not gone and dwelt by faith
in that land, their seed would never have inherited it, and the
purpose of God could not have been fulfilled. Bethlehem had to
be built and possessed by the seed of Abraham, as indeed
Nazareth and Capernaum. Jerusalem had to be possessed to
become the capital of the kingdom, and the temple had to be
built within it. In Jacob's day, there were no people of God in
the land other than his immediate family. Thus we can see how

the very meaning and significance of Jacob's life and calling
were centered in the promised land. How the powers of
darkness must have sought in every way possible to compromise Jacob and thus neutralize the purpose of God. After all,
the focal point of everything in the purpose of God was the
coming of the Messiah. In Him everything relating to God's
purpose for time and eternity was centered.

Jacob's love for the land

Christians often speak about Abraham and Isaac as if they were
both incredible saints with hardly a fault. It is, however, a point
to make that all the deceit and cunning did not originate with
Rebecca. Preachers sometimes speak as if all the twistedness
came from her and Laban's side of the family. There is no doubt
that there was a twistedness in them. The fact is that Terah,
Abraham's father, was the great-grandfather also of Laban and
Rebecca. Even in Abraham there was this streak of deceit. After
all, he went down into Egypt in unbelief. It was a lapse of faith.
He did not go down to Egypt because the Lord appeared to him
and commanded him to go. He lent on his own understanding
and, out of fear that the Lord could not provide food, he went.
When he arrived in Egypt, he called his wife, who was his half-
sister, his sister, and brought upon himself tremendous trouble
(see Gen. 12:10–20). Pharaoh could have executed him, and
then there would have been no Isaac and no Jacob. It is even
more remarkable that Abraham made the same mistake again
(see Gen. 20:1–18). It is clear that it was not only Jacob who had
this streak of deceit within him.

Remarkable as it may seem, Isaac, who everybody seems
to consider a saint and incapable of anything twisted, was
ensnared in the same way. He called his wife, Rebecca, his sister
(see Gen. 26:1–11). At least he did not go down into Egypt but
remained within the land in spite of the famine, and experienced the prosperous blessing of the Lord.

Whatever we feel about Jacob he never spoke of either Leah or Rachel as his sister, nor did he ever consider living outside the borders of the covenanted and promised land, although strictly speaking Haran was not within the borders of that land. Nevertheless, he did not choose to live in Haran but was fleeing for his life from Esau. Whereas the Lord had to speak to his father Isaac to *prevent* him from going down to Egypt, the Lord had to *command* Jacob to go down. It would *never* have entered his head. He was the only one of the three patriarchs who would have never considered such a possibility.

Jacob may have had many problems with the strength of his own nature, with his self-will, with his fleshly zeal to get things done, but he had a deep regard for the things of God. Deeper than his twistedness, than his deceit, than his business acumen and shrewdness, was this desire for the things of God. He wanted the birthright because he valued it. That was the principal reason. It was also the reason that he stole the blessing. He recognized the preciousness of it. He understood God's promise about the land, and when famine came to the whole area and there was plenty of food in Egypt, he was not prepared to journey down there. He preferred to remain in the land, in spite of famine, believing that God would meet his needs, as he trusted and obeyed Him. It is true that if it had been the will of God for him to remain in the land, the Lord would have kept him and honored him. After all, many years later the Lord kept Elijah alive in a time of famine and drought by feeding him through ravens and giving him water to drink through a little brook. In this instance, however, it was the purpose of God that Jacob should go down into Egypt, for there the Lord purposed to birth a nation.

And God spake unto Israel in the visions of the night, and said, Jacob, Jacob. And he said, Here am I. And he said, I am God, the God of thy father: fear not to go down into Egypt; for I will there make of thee a great nation: I will go down with thee into Egypt; and I will also surely bring thee up again ...

(Gen. 46:2–4)

Our Promised Land – Christ

All of this may be true and factual but what can we, as believers, as members of the body of the Messiah, learn from it? In my estimation we have in the promised land a very clearly defined picture or type of that "so great salvation" which alone is found in and through the Messiah Jesus.

A land of covenant

In Christ, in the Messiah Jesus, God covenants to give us everything.

> Now the God of peace, who brought again from the dead the great shepherd of the sheep with the blood of an eternal covenant, even our Lord Jesus, make you perfect in every good thing to do his will, working in us that which is well-pleasing in his sight, through Jesus Christ ...
>
> (Heb. 13:20–21a)

It is an eternal covenant that God has made with us, and it is sealed with nothing less than the blood of our Lord Jesus. Within that eternal covenant God has given us everything necessary to enable us and to equip us to do His will. He holds nothing back!

> He that spared not his own Son, but delivered him up for us all, how shall he not also with him freely give us all things?
>
> (Rom. 8:32)

All the fullness, the unsearchable riches, the infinite extent of His salvation, is given to us in the Messiah!

The promised land was given to the children of Israel on the basis of the Passover lamb slain in Egypt. Through the death of the lamb, the whole land was theirs to "possess." It is the same with us. God gives us everything on the basis of the slain Lamb. It is the finished work of the Lord Jesus which guarantees that all is ours in Him. The simple but extraordinary truth is that God Himself has entered into an eternal covenant with those He saves, and it is sealed by the blood of the Messiah.

A land of provision – everything in Christ

God has given us a promised land and within it He gives us everything! Outside of that land He promises nothing. In other words, He covenants to give us everything in the Lord Jesus and nothing apart from Him. Every single and necessary thing to turn a sinner into a saint is provided in Christ; all the grace needed to transform our character and to change us into His likeness is provided. In Him and by Him the Holy Spirit enables us to live a full Christian life. Everything we need for service is also provided within Christ: the anointing, the power, the gifts, and the equipment are all ours in Him.

In the same way in which everything needed for national life, for family life, for business life, and for personal life was provided in that land, so it is with Christ. In Him God gives us everything.

> for in him dwelleth all the fullness of the Godhead bodily, and in him ye are made full [complete]...
>
> (Col. 2:9–10a)

And again,

> For it was the good pleasure of the Father that in him should all the fulness dwell...
>
> (Col. 1:19)

Note carefully that "in Him we are made complete."

Everything that is required for us to reach the divine goal is provided in Him. We have to learn to abide in Christ, if we are to reach the end of the Lord. In the same way that the children of Israel had to dwell in the land and refuse any attempt to compromise them, or draw them out of it, we must learn the same lesson. If we will possess our possessions, if by the Spirit of God we discover what is ours in Christ and lay hold of it, by His grace we shall come to His goal.

There is much that was hidden from the eye in that land, for example: the iron and the copper. It had to be discovered and mined. There were times when to the eye the land did not flow with milk and honey, but when the rains came everything changed. All the deep wells and lakes filled up, water flowed everywhere, and the whole land became alive with flowers and greenery; out of that water came all the fruitfulness.

Many a time believers are tempted to leave the land and go down to "Egypt," or go to "Babylon," for in them it seems that there is plenty of everything necessary for a full life. In the promised land, everything seems difficult, if not at times impossible. One can still go to Egypt or Babylon and be a child of God; one can be saved even if you live there or somewhere else, but one will never know His fullness. One can even have homes and families, and build meeting places in Babylon, worshiping the Lord, and studying the Word of God, as the Jews did. However, the city of God cannot be built there, nor can the Messiah be born there. For that to be fulfilled, the land had to be possessed by those that would dwell in it.

It is the same with us. You and I cannot reach the end of the Lord, we cannot grow to maturity unless we dwell in Christ. If you and I are to be the bride of Christ, those materials out of which alone she is built, gold, precious stone, and pearl, are only to be found in Him. As we abide in Christ, and He in us, that life and nature of His becomes in us the material for the city of God.

Consider also the declaration of the apostle Paul:

> Blessed be the God and Father of our Lord Jesus Christ, who hath blessed us with every spiritual blessing in the heavenly places in Christ...
>
> (Eph. 1:3)

Where do we find all the blessings promised to us by God? They are all in the Messiah. They are not found outside of Him. In Him there is "a land" full of blessings; you cannot experience them all at once. If we did, we could not contain them. These blessings are not an ideal but a reality, and the Lord knows how much we can experience at any single moment in our lives. Note carefully that it is "every spiritual blessing." There is no spiritual blessing that is not given to us in the Lord Jesus. The Word of God is full of the description of these blessings, and every one of them is ours in the Messiah.

Then again, the apostle Paul writing to the Philippians states,

> And my God shall supply every need of yours according to his riches in glory in Christ Jesus.
>
> (Phil. 4:19)

We should be careful to note that these needs are not just spiritual needs but every kind of need known to man. This covers the whole gamut of need – spiritual, mental, physical, and material. What a promise given to us by the Spirit of God through the apostle! The Lord longs to "make known the riches of His glory upon vessels of mercy afore prepared unto glory." Are you a vessel of mercy? Then to you He wants to make the riches of His glory known. Generally speaking He uses the needs in our lives to drive us into a deeper experience of Him. When we are in great need, it is in that moment that we find no alternative will suffice but a new and fuller experience of Him; we discover that, in Him, God supplies whatever need we may have. Then we realize that the purpose of God for us is intimately and directly bound up with the Lord Jesus, with our dwelling in Him and His dwelling in us.

Is it any wonder that the apostle Paul prayed so fervently for the saints?

> For this cause I bow my knees unto the Father ... that ye ... may be strong to apprehend with all the saints what is the breadth and length and height and depth, and to know the love of Christ which passeth knowledge, that ye may be filled unto all the fulness of God.
>
> (Eph. 3:14, 18–19)

Here is a land to be discovered in which everything required for the fulfillment of God's purpose is found, whether personal or corporate.

A land to be possessed

For some people it is hard to recognize this land as a picture of our "so great salvation" in the Messiah. They read of wars and conflict, and many enemies that withstand the possession of the land. Indeed, before the land was won, there were fierce conflicts and many wars fought over it and within it. There is, however, no way in which the land can be possessed, and the purpose of God fulfilled, without such conflict. The powers of darkness will contend every step of the way, seeking to compromise us, to demoralize us, and in the end to defeat us. At the very least, they will seek to make us settle for something less than the whole counsel of God and His full purpose. The simplest believer knows from experience that the moment he begins to follow the Lord Jesus, Satan is out to divert him from that path and will use every means available to compromise him. We discover that we have been born into a war, and a war not of our making.

To use the illustration of the land, if the enemy of God cannot keep the children of Israel in Egypt, he will use the "Egypt" in them to unsettle them and become the impetus for them to return to it. For children of God to live in Egypt is a contradiction to the very meaning of their salvation and deliverance. It is true that you can certainly experience divine deliverance from the powers of darkness: the angel of death cannot touch you because of the blood of the Lamb. However, you cannot experience the full meaning of being transferred into the kingdom of His dear Son, unless you dwell in the land (see Col. 1:13). Likewise, one can experience the pillar of cloud and fire leading the people of God in the wilderness; the promise of manna, the bread of life; the water miraculously coming out of the rock; the diseases of Egypt not touching them; and their clothes and their sandals not wearing out. Nevertheless, it was an endless circuit of experiencing the acts of the Lord and the grace of God, and at the same time a complete ignorance of His ways. His acts anyone can see. To understand His ways is to be in another dimension! That circuit lasted forty years, and that generation never arrived at the fulfillment of His purpose, for which they had been delivered out of Egypt. So many Christian believers are "experiencing" but never arriving! It is so easy to settle down to something less than God's full purpose, and Satan's main activity is to waylay the believer and neutralize the grace of God in him or in her.

To be possessed by faith

In the Eternal Covenant that God has made with us and sealed by the blood of the Lord Jesus, He promises not only to save us, but with the Lord Jesus He promises to give us everything. In it He makes us His heirs and joint heirs with the Messiah. If it were not in the Word of God, it would be incredible. Our basic problem is an evil heart of unbelief. What God has

promised us in the Lord Jesus, has to be possessed by practical
and living faith. The Lord said to Joshua,

> Every place that the sole of your foot shall tread upon, to you
> have I given it ...
>
> (Josh. 1:3)

In fact, the boundaries of the promised land were defined
by God, but only that which the children of God possessed by
faith, became theirs in reality. He had said:

> For mine angel shall go before thee, and bring thee in unto the
> Amorite, and the Hittite, and the Perizzite, and the Canaanite,
> the Hivite, and the Jebusite: and I will cut them off ... I will
> send my terror before thee, and will discomfit all the people to
> whom thou shalt come, and I will make all thine enemies turn
> their backs unto thee. And I will send the hornet before thee,
> which shall drive out the Hivite, the Canaanite, and the
> Hittite, from before thee.
>
> (Exod. 23:23, 27–28)

It must have seemed to many of the children of Israel that
there would be no battle; the Lord would have driven out all the
enemies before they arrived. That is the wrong idea of God's
predestinating power and purpose. One can imagine some of the
people of God saying, "The angel of the Lord is going to go
before us and do it all. The Passover Lamb sacrificed for us is the
basis for our deliverance, for our redemption, and for our being a
nation. The Jordan will have parted before we arrive, and the
walls of the cities will have fallen down before we have even
come to them."

As it was with the children of Israel, so it is the same with us.
We believe that everything is ours in the Lord Jesus and that we
do not need to do anything. It is a finished work. This is
absolutely true and there can be no argument about that: the

work of our salvation is complete – there is nothing to be added. Nevertheless, unless you and I *possess by faith* what the Lord Jesus has won for us, it does not become our experience.

The soles of your feet

The children of Israel had to use the soles of their feet, and then the angel of the Lord did everything. He was poised to fulfill all that God had promised for His children, but until by faith they used the "soles of their feet," he did nothing. It is the same with us. We know nothing of the fulfillment of His promises, until by faith we possess them. So much is promised in the salvation which is ours in the Lord Jesus, but it is only when we trust and obey that we experience the reality.

The words of the apostle Paul are an invaluable commentary on this:

> work out your own salvation with fear and trembling; for it is God who worketh in you both to will and to work, for his good pleasure.
>
> (Phil. 2:12b–13)

Unless you work out your salvation, God does not work in you both to will and to work. In the testimony of Paul later in this letter, he basically states the same truth:

> I press on, if so be that I may lay hold on that for which also I was laid hold on by Christ Jesus.
>
> (Phil. 3:12)

It is a very strong word he uses in Greek, meaning "to arrest" or "to apprehend." It is the same spiritual idea, whether we describe it as putting the soles of our feet down on promised land, or possessing what the Lord has already won for us, or laying hold on that for which Christ has laid hold on us. If we do not possess what has already been won for us in our so great salvation, we stand to lose much.

Faith and patience

The writer of the letter to the Hebrews exhorts us to "be not sluggish, but imitators of them who through faith and patience inherit the promises" (6:12). Sometimes the moment we exercise living faith, the Lord moves into action, and it happens immediately. Such was the experience of the children of Israel when they came to the Jordan. The moment the feet of the priests, bearing the Ark of the Covenant, touched the riverbed (they got their feet wet), the river parted and the children of Israel went over as on dry land. However, when they came to Jericho, the order was that they were to walk around the city once a day for six days, and on the seventh day they were to walk around it seven times. One can imagine that many of the children of God questioned whether this was not unbelief. Why would it require all this walking around the city, especially seven times on the seventh day, when the Lord had instantly fulfilled His promise with the river Jordan? Was the Lord tired?

It was divine wisdom that gave the command, "no talking, no shouting, and no blowing of trumpets until the end of the seventh circuit." This is divine psychology in action. I have seen so many prayer times destroyed by endless talking and discussion! The more we all talk, the greater the problems become until, in confusion, unbelief, and weakness, we begin to pray. Such prayer times never arrive anywhere.

To inherit the promises sometimes requires only faith, but other times it requires faith *and patience*. Why the Lord wanted them to go round the city so many times, only He knows, but it was surely for our instruction. The only way we can see the fulfillment of the purpose of God in our lives, personally or corporately, is when we learn to obey His instructions.

It is interesting to note that the possession of Jerusalem only became fact some four hundred years later. Apparently the children of God were disorientated by the strength of the Jebusites and the fact that there were iron chariots in the area. The inhabitants seemed so invincible and Jerusalem so impregnable. Actually the children of Israel only had to use the soles of their feet and the Lord would have gone into action, and Jerusalem would have been theirs. Satan had a vested interest in keeping Jerusalem out of their hands. After all it was Jerusalem that was divinely destined to be the capital of the kingdom and the place where the house of the Lord was to be built. Only when David's men used the soles of their feet many years later and climbed up the shaft from the spring Gihon, did the Lord give the city to them. The shaft, it should be noted, was within the city walls!

From all of this we learn some tremendous lessons. Through the finished work of the Lamb, there is no problem that cannot be solved, no difficulty that cannot be overcome, and no advance that cannot be made. No enemy, however fierce or powerful, can nullify, or neutralize, the purpose of God for a life that He has saved, or for the church for which He has such future plans, or for the service and work to which He has called us. The conflict may be enormous and continuous but it cannot prevent the fulfillment of God's will and word. Nevertheless, the Lord will not move into action until we exercise practical and living faith.

We have to learn to use the keys of the kingdom, not presumptuously or arrogantly but under His direction and in fellowship with other believers. Then the Lord builds *His* Church and the gates of hell are unable to destroy that building work. It is another way of saying that we have to use the soles of our feet. There is no alternative if we are to possess our inheritance and see the fulfillment of the purpose of God.

Entering into the land

To us has been given the Word of God and it is through faith and patience that we inherit the promises. We have to take the

Word of God, as the Holy Spirit enlightens us and applies it to our day and generation and to our circumstances, and claim its fulfillment.

> Let us fear therefore, lest haply, a promise being left of entering into his rest [that is the land where all is provided and not the wilderness], any one of you should seem to have come short of it. For indeed we have had good tidings [the gospel] preached unto us, even as also they: but the word of hearing did not profit them, because it was not united by faith . . .
>
> (Heb. 4:1–2)

Those who belong to the Lord often feel that what He has promised cannot or does not work for *them*. They believe that the special and unique problems, or complex difficulties, confronting them, make them an exception to the divine rule. It is a deep-seated sense that what works for others will not work for us. Many a servant of God has the same problem with his or her calling and work.

There are not a few Christians who believe that the Lord would never speak to them. They cannot believe that the Father would speak to them personally, that He would take His Word and personally apply it to them, to their lives and circumstances. It would be strange if a human father never spoke to his son or to his daughter: how much more our Father in heaven! The Lord Jesus emphasized this when He said, "My sheep hear My voice." The fact is that the Lord longs to speak to those who are His children and there is much in the Word of God about the necessity of spiritual hearing. Unfortunately there is a popular idea that to hear the Lord, a person must be born a mystic. Many times one hears it said, "I am a very practical man; I have never heard God's voice, and I never will." Some doctors tell us that when we are young and do not want to hear, we can develop deafness. *Many Christians have become deaf through unbelief or an unreadiness to obey the Lord.*

I should state, on the other hand, that many believers are afraid of this matter because of the Christian cranks who continuously speak about "what the Lord is saying to them." Such people are either mentally unstable or spiritually deceived. It is not the Lord who is speaking to them at all, but often their own soul, and sometimes evil spirits.

We should note carefully the second half of verse 2, "the word of hearing did not profit them because it was not united by faith." One can hear or read, or even study the Word of God and not *hear* the Lord. There is no outcome or consequence; no experience of its reality. The reason for this condition is simple. The Word of God was not united to them through living faith. It is practical faith, a faith that works, which brings fulfillment. Where there is such faith the word of Christ *dwells* in us richly; we are receiving the *implanted* word (see Col. 3:16; Jas 1:21).

Jacob and this promised land

The Lord had confirmed with Jacob the covenant He had made with his grandfather and father in which He had promised the land of Canaan as an everlasting possession to them and to their seed. The problem was not Jacob's hearing. Jacob had heard the Lord and believed Him. The problem was Jacob!

He was a man with such strength of natural character, such fleshly zeal, and such untiring energy that he could not leave anything to the Lord. He had to supervise the Lord's work and make sure that it was fulfilled. Men and women who have this kind of powerful soul energy are unable to wait for the Lord. If the Lord does not work, they will work for Him, with disastrous consequences. We see this clearly in Jacob. In the work that God wanted to do, Jacob was a trial to Him. Spontaneously and unconsciously, he was an obstacle to the fulfillment of God's purpose. Indeed, it was the abounding grace of God that brought Jacob to that fulfillment, in spite of his own efforts to work it. We must always remember that working *with* God is vastly different to working *for* God. When you work *with* the Lord, you are under His supervision and empowered by His strength. When you work *for* the Lord, you "do your own thing" and seek *His* support.

Jacob stole his twin brother's birthright by a clever deal and took away his blessing by deceiving his nearly blind and godly old father. We have no record of a repentant Jacob, although I am sure that he was deeply sorry for *himself.* He suffered so much from his own actions. He is described as a home-lover and had to leave his home; he loved and valued his mother and had to leave her, never again to see her. For twenty years he suffered his uncle Laban's dealings with him, until he saw himself in Laban.

Exhausted with the events of leaving his family and his home, he lay down to sleep with a stone for a pillow. It was at that point of sorrow and confusion that the Lord appeared to him with a vision of incredible significance (Gen. 28:10–22). The Lord never rebuked him, nor demanded of him that he repent. Even when Jacob began to bargain with the Lord (vv. 20–22), the Lord did not turn away from him. The strength of Jacob's soul life is revealed clearly in this incident; he could not forego a deal. The Lord, however, knew that He would have to wait for years before a deep and full work could be done in him. In the meantime the Lord spoke to him with incredible love and grace. Is there anyone like the Lord? If God could appear to a man in a condition like that, with a character like that, would He not speak also to you?

Chapter 5

A People and a Blessing

In this chapter, we will deal with two more lessons from the life of Jacob. Both of them are essential. The first is Jacob becoming a people, and the second is Jacob becoming a blessing.

Jacob Becomes a People

Another vital aspect of the purpose of God for Jacob was that he should become the father of a nation, that a people should be reproduced through him. It is the principle of fruitfulness and multiplication.

> And thy seed shall be as the dust of the earth, and thou shalt spread abroad to the west, and to the east, and to the north, and to the south. And in thee and in thy seed shall all the families of the earth be blessed.
>
> (Gen. 28:14)

> And God said unto him, I am God Almighty: be fruitful and multiply; a nation and a company of nations shall be of thee, and kings shall come out of thy loins.
>
> (Gen. 35:11)

God's purpose for His own never changes. It is that we should be fruitful and multiply. At the very beginning of the human story the Lord said, "It is not good that the man should be alone," and created woman (see Gen. 2:18). The Lord's purpose was that together they should produce a family, and become a people. It is significant therefore that the first words God spoke to man, as recorded in the Bible, were, "Be fruitful, and multiply" (Gen. 1:28). Or again, when the whole human race was destroyed in a flood, except for eight people, it is recorded that the Lord said to the survivors: "be fruitful, and multiply" (Gen. 8:17; 9:1). Centuries later when God appeared to Abraham, at that point childless, He said,

> for all the land which thou seest, to thee will I give it, and to thy seed forever. And I will make thy seed as the dust of the earth: So that if a man can number the dust of the earth, then may thy seed also be numbered.
>
> (Gen. 13:15–16)

And again,

> And he [the LORD] brought him forth abroad, and said, Look now toward heaven, and number the stars, if thou be able to number them: and he said unto him, So shall thy seed be.
>
> (Gen. 15:5)

The Lord's concern for fruitfulness and multiplication

There is no part of the divine record where the Lord is not concerned about fruitfulness and multiplication. It is also interesting to note that wherever the Lord made such promises of fruitfulness and multiplication, Satan tried to create barrenness. Again and again the Lord had to work by a miracle. Sarah, Rebecca, and Hannah are examples of such miracles.

Isaiah could almost be called the prophet of fruitfulness and multiplication. For instance:

> Sing O barren, thou that didst not bear; break forth into singing, and cry aloud, thou that didst not travail with child: for more are the children of the desolate than the children of the married wife, saith the LORD. Enlarge the place of thy tent, and let them stretch forth the curtains of thy habitations; spare not: lengthen thy cords, and strengthen thy stakes. For thou shalt spread abroad on the right hand and on the left; and thy seed shall possess the nations, and make the desolate cities to be inhabited.
>
> (Isa. 54:1–3)

And again:

> But Zion said, the LORD hath forsaken me, and the Lord hath forgotten me. Can a woman forget her sucking child, that she should not have compassion on the son of her womb? Yea, these may forget, yet will not I forget thee … For, as for thy waste and thy desolate places, and thy land that hath been destroyed, surely now shalt thou be too strait for the inhabitants, and they that swallowed thee up shall be far away. The children of thy bereavement shall yet say in thine ears, The place is too strait for me; give place to me that I may dwell. Then shalt thou say in thy heart, Who hath begotten me these, seeing I have been bereaved of my children, and am solitary, an exile, and wandering to and fro? and who hath brought up these? Behold, I was left alone; these, where were they?
>
> (Isa. 49:14–15, 19–21)

It is all summed up when Isaiah declared:

> The little one shall become a thousand, and the small one a strong nation: I, the LORD, will hasten it in its time.
>
> (Isa. 60:22)

This was certainly true of Abraham, of Isaac, and of Jacob; and these prophecies are having a literal fulfillment in our day and generation in the recreation of the state of Israel.

The principle that lies at the heart of all of this is simple. God purposes that we should be fruitful and multiply. How sad it is when we, as Christians, have never been responsible for another human being finding God. We become a sad contradiction of His purpose for us. The Lord Jesus put it simply:

> Ye did not choose me but I chose you, and appointed you, that ye should go and bear fruit, and that your fruit should abide: that whatsoever ye shall ask of the Father in my name, he may give it you.
>
> (John 15:16)

In fact, the whole of this discourse in John 15 is concerned with fruitfulness. Many will point out that this is the fruit of the Spirit: love, joy, peace, longsuffering, kindness, goodness, faithfulness, meekness, and self-control. There is no problem with that viewpoint, for wherever the fruit of the Spirit is in evidence, unsaved men and women are saved. We must always remember that within the fruit is the seed of reproduction and multiplication.

The Word of God grew and multiplied

It seems to me a strange position that some Christians take when they pour scorn upon any evangelistic concern or outreach; when such a burden is considered to reveal shallowness and lack of spiritual depth. The mentality expressed by such an attitude is that everything related to reaching the unsaved and bringing them to Christ is kindergarten. Apparently, those who are advancing in the purpose of God, and in their experience of Him, must leave such matters behind them. Such an attitude is totally foreign to the Lord, and to the Word of God. You cannot divide experiencing the deeper things of God, and having an understanding of the Church and God's eternal purpose, from deep travail and burden for the unsaved. Many, however, make such a division and, in so doing, bring a spiritual staleness and death upon themselves. Is it possible to follow the Lord closely and not feel the concern of His heart? Evangelistic concern is not kindergarten but is a genuine expression of the heart of the Lord. In my estimation it is not possible to be joined to the Lord in one Spirit and not have in us His burden for a dying world.

It is a fact that in both the physical and spiritual worlds you cannot have birth without conception and travail. Genuine travail must begin with the Holy Spirit conceiving in our spirit a burden, which in turn becomes a painful anguish in intercession for the unsaved. When evangelism begins in the Lord, its end will always be fruit and multiplication.

In the book of Acts we read,

> And the word of God increased; and the number of the disciples multiplied in Jerusalem exceedingly ...
>
> (Acts 6:7)

And again,

> But the word of God grew and multiplied.
>
> (Acts 12:24)

How can the Word of God increase? How can it grow? The way Luke records this is arresting and challenging. Surely it can only mean that the Word of God increases in us; it grows in us. The result is always the same: it is multiplication. The tragedy is that in so many believers, and in so many assemblies, the Word of God grows only in our heads and not in our hearts. The consequence is that there is no multiplication but only stagnation.

What I have said is no justification for the type of evangelism in which the flesh and the world are in action and not the Spirit of

God. Sometimes methods and techniques are used which belong to the world of mass-psychology and manipulation, and are not His work. There are practices that are used in some instances which are even fraudulent, especially in relation to finances. It brings evangelism into reproach but in no way invalidates the command of the Lord that we should "go into all the world and preach the gospel to every creature" (Mark 16:15 NKJV).

The path to the fulfillment of God-given burden

In the way that the Lord speaks of Jacob in Isaiah we see this purpose of God for fruitfulness and multiplication:

> But now thus saith the LORD that created thee, O Jacob, and he that formed thee, O Israel: Fear not, for I have redeemed thee; I have called thee by thy name, thou art mine. When thou passest through the waters, I will be with thee; and through the rivers, they shall not overflow thee: when thou walkest through the fire, thou shalt not be burned, neither shall the flame kindle upon thee.
>
> (Isa. 43:1–2)

In the experience of the redeeming work of the Lord in our lives, there will be many trials. There are waters and even rivers to pass through; fire and flame to endure. If we follow the Lord the path lies through such experiences. There is no way to avoid them. In previous chapters I have already mentioned this matter, and the point I am restating is that we have to *pass through them* to the goal that the Lord has in mind. That end is fruitfulness and multiplication.

Consider how He continues to speak:

> For I am the LORD thy God, the Holy One of Israel, thy Saviour; I have given Egypt as thy ransom, Ethiopia and Seba in thy stead. Since thou hast been precious in my sight, and

honorable, and I have loved thee; therefore will I give men in thy stead, and peoples instead of thy life. Fear not; for I am with thee: I will bring thy seed from the east, and gather thee from the west; I will say to the north, Give up; and to the south, Keep not back; bring my sons from far, and my daughters from the end of the earth; every one that is called by my name, and whom I have created for my glory, whom I have formed, yea, whom I have made.

(Isa. 43:3–7)

What a wonderful aim the Lord has! He begins with a Jacob and ends with a nation. He begins with many trials and much anguish, and ends in Jacob's seed coming from the four corners of the earth into the glory of God. Never ignore or shelve this matter, for it lies at the heart of God's purpose for Jacob. It lies at the heart of His purpose for you and for me. It is divine multiplication. The one becomes a thousand, the small one a strong nation. When this happens, it is the Lord's doing and can only be marvelous in our eyes. Nevertheless, the question has to be asked, "Are you ready for the necessary travail? Are you ready for the spiritual pain and anguish in your spirit? Are you ready to lay down your life for the Lord's sake and for the gospel?"

The beauty of God's grace toward Jacob is seen in the fact that he had all but one of his twelve sons and his one daughter *before* he was changed into Israel. They were the beginning of the nation God purposed to create. Where would we be if God refused to touch us until we were changed into His likeness? Truly, the Lord sees the end from the beginning and deals with us, in mercy and in grace, as if His goal had already been reached in us.

Jacob Becomes a Blessing

Yet another vital aspect of God's purpose for Jacob was that he should be a blessing to others. Jacob was anything but a blessing! He was not a giver: he was an acquirer. He did not bless his twin brother: he stole the blessing from him. He did not bless his aged father: he deceived him. He did not even bless Rebecca, whom he loved dearly: she never saw him again. I am not sure that in the end she thought of that as a blessing. He did not bless Laban: according to Laban he stole his flocks and his two daughters. Jacob could not help it, he was always acquiring. No one in his or her right mind would have ever described him as a blessing.

As I have already pointed out, Jacob is sometimes represented as an effeminate, spineless man – an indoor type. However, Jacob was, mentally, an infinitely tougher man than Esau. His hard and tough nature came out when he refused to give the exhausted and ravenous Esau one ladle of the stew he was cooking, until he agreed to sell his birthright. It seems he would have held out until Esau died of hunger, unless he "signed on the dotted line"! Jacob was a tough character. He had a soul-strength, an iron-like will, and an unbelievably sharp and calculating shrewdness of mind. He had boundless natural energy and resources. The problem was that he was totally unaware of himself and "did what came naturally." Many of us come into this category. Jacob perfectly describes us: self-centered, self-seeking, and self-fulfilling. The interesting fact is that, like Jacob, we are totally unaware of it.

There for the blessing, not to bless

The whole life of such children of God is centered on what can be acquired. They are not givers but acquirers. They will go from fellowship to fellowship, from place to place, always receiving and never giving. Everything is judged on what they receive rather than what they give. They are there for the blessing and not to bless. They come into Christian work or a company of believers and expect everything to revolve around them. Such Christians are not a blessing to others; they steal the blessing from others. In some measure all of us come into this category, and our problem is the same as with Jacob. It is the strength of our will, of our soul, of our natural energy: it is self-centeredness. We are, of course, unaware of ourselves. Everyone else is only too aware of us! Left to ourselves we would spoil and ruin everything!

I will not let you go, except you bless me!

It was only when Jacob was desperate, and the Lord met him and wrestled with him, that a cry was torn out of the innermost part of his being, "I will not let you go, except you bless me." Clearly, this was not the use of the word "blessing" so often found amongst Christian believers! Genuine self-revelation had devastated Jacob. Nothing would satisfy him other than an experience that left him a changed man. Out of the depths of his desperation was born a determination. The kind of blessing with which God blessed Jacob cost him his self-life! It transformed him and made him a blessing to others.

Jacob becomes a blessing to others

The Lord worked so deeply in this man that, at the end of his life, he gave again and again. He became a blessing. Even to one of the greatest potentates in antiquity, the Pharaoh of Egypt, Jacob became a blessing. It is a wonderful story that is recorded in Genesis 47 when the aged Jacob lifted up his hands and blessed Pharaoh. It was a genuine blessing. In fact, he blessed Pharaoh twice (vv. 7, 10). As Jacob lay dying, he blessed the two sons of Joseph. He blessed them in such a noteworthy manner that the Hebrew letter records it as one of the high points of his life (11:21).

In Genesis 49 we have Jacob's blessing upon each of his twelve sons. What a work the Lord had worked in Jacob that he could bless each of them. Before Jabbok he could never have blessed anyone. Now in words of incredible beauty, the aged and transformed Jacob becomes the vehicle of blessing for each of his sons. It is a remarkable record. When you read his blessing of Reuben and of Simeon and of Levi, it is not what we would normally understand as a blessing. It is neither sentimental nor even "nice," but straightforward and truthful. Nevertheless, it was a blessing. It was as if he, with the eye of God, saw into the very heart and character of his sons. He understood them because now he understood himself. In knowing himself, he knew that God's faithfulness towards him would be the same faithfulness that God would also show them.

God's purpose that we should be a blessing

In truth, has any child of God not been blessed through Jacob? I think not. Every one of us has been blessed through him. By the grace of God we have been brought into the salvation of God, into the life of God, into all the blessings of God, and into the purpose of God. The twister, the supplanter, the one who stole the blessings, has become the one who blesses us all. From this we learn one simple but profound lesson. It is the purpose of God that every one of His children should become a blessing and, in becoming such a blessing, should win others to the Lord. This matter is directly linked to fruitfulness and multiplication. It has, however, always to be remembered that to become a blessing to others, a spiritual history with the Lord is necessary. It requires direct experience of Him that is costly, and a readiness for the Holy Spirit to deal with us in painful and practical ways.

It is also the purpose of God that we should become a blessing to others in encouragement, in comfort, in fellowship, and in forbearing love. The Word of God is full of exhortations over this matter.

What does it mean that we should "build one another up in love"? To build up the body of Christ, to build up one another, we surely have to be a blessing. Can I be a blessing? Can you be a blessing? We can only be a blessing to others if first we have something of the Lord to give. Before the Lord dealt with Jacob at Jabbok, he left a trail of damage wherever he went. It is a terrible thought that we could be a curse to others. However, if our self-life, and the poison of the serpent within it, has not been dealt a death blow, it is a dread possibility. Indeed, this describes many a situation in the work of God, and in the Church of God. No child of God would want to be a curse, or to leave a trail of damage wherever they go. The problem is that like Jacob we are unaware of the dark potentialities in our self-life. Only when that self-life is laid down, are we safe. Then, and only then, can we become a blessing. Is this not the way to blessing and multiplication?

Chapter 6

Divine Authority

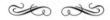

Power with God and Power with Man

It was always the purpose of the Lord that Jacob should rule. In the prophecy given to Rebecca, his mother, it is clear: "The elder shall serve the younger" (Gen. 25:23); and in the prophecy uttered by Isaac:

> Let peoples serve thee, And nations bow down to thee. Be lord over thy brethren, And let thy mother's sons bow down to thee.
>
> (Gen. 27:29)

God never intended Jacob to be at the mercy of his circumstances and his situations; or at the mercy of other human beings; or even at the mercy of the enemies of the purpose of God. From the beginning it was God's will that Jacob should have "power with God and with men." It was certainly not His will that Jacob should be bound by Jacob and therefore useless to Him. His purpose was that Jacob should become Israel, a prince with God. He wanted to bring him to the throne, where with the Lord he should reign. Here in Jacob's life and experience we discover yet another lesson, a lesson that is hard for many of us to learn!

Jacob's wrong kind of power

The problem was that Jacob had the wrong kind of power coming from the wrong kind of source! The only way in which he had power with men was to manipulate them, engineering their circumstances to his advantage. The natural strength of his mind and will, his acute business acumen, the ability to scent a bargain and strike a deal, all combined to give him power with others. So strong was this mindset that when the Lord appeared to him at Bethel, he even bargained with Him:

> If God will be with me, and will keep me in this way that I go, and will give me bread to eat, and raiment to put on, so that I come again to my father's house in peace, then the LORD will be my God, and this stone, which I have set up for a pillar, shall be God's house. And of all that thou shalt give me I will surely give the tenth to thee.
>
> (Gen. 28:20–22 mg)

One can almost sense the atmosphere from the divine record! Jacob's words betray his attitude, even if he was not conscious of it. "The Lord should feel Himself greatly blessed and helped by His relationship to me. He should be thankful to me for my support and graciousness."

When one considers that Jacob was in fact fleeing from his twin brother and his father's home in disgrace, it is amazing to recognize the powerful strength of Jacob's nature. He was clearly unaware of it. Normally one would expect that if the Lord appeared to a man in such circumstances, he would be prostrate on his face before the Lord in brokenness and repentance. Not so with Jacob! The Lord had confirmed the covenant which He had made with Abraham and Isaac, and then had added specific promises to Jacob. Jacob's reaction was to make the most of the Lord's promises, and sought to strike a bargain! The bargain which Jacob sought was for his own well-being, security, and prosperity! In a somewhat condescending manner, he said he would even "build a house for the Lord" around the stone he had used as a pillar! What happened, one wonders, with the promised tithe? Did Jacob keep his promise or did he conveniently forget it? We have no further knowledge of what transpired over it.

In one sense you could say that Jacob had power with God even then in his unbroken state. The power he had with God was that God loved him, and was prepared to allow Jacob to "manipulate" Him. He knew exactly what Jacob was seeking to do. The Lord understood his game and decided "to play along with him." He knew that in the end Jacob would come to Jabbok and would become Israel.

Jacob the prince of God

When, at Jabbok, the Lord gave Jacob a new name He said,

> Thy name shall be called no more Jacob, but Israel: for thou hast striven with God and with men, and hast prevailed.
>
> (Gen. 32:28)

The meaning of the name "Israel" is deeply significant and full of beauty. It could be translated a number of ways. It could be interpreted as "prince of God," because the root idea in it is "to have power." Some of the more modern versions translate the name as either "God strives" or "He who strives with God." It probably contains all these ideas. God did strive with Jacob and Jacob did strive with God, and the result was a man with divine authority, a prince of God! According to a number of Hebrew authorities there is a play on words between the Hebrew words *Elohim* (God, the Almighty, the Infinite) and *anashim* (man, finite and weak). It is interesting to note that both the Greek of the LXX and the Latin of the Vulgate read, "for thou has prevailed with God, and shall be mighty with men." If this is true, then we should understand the meaning of God's words to be, "Seeing you have had power with the Infinite Almighty, you will surely also have power with finite man"!

Jacob's power with God and therefore with men

Jacob surely had a kind of power with men but it was the wrong sort of power. Now he is told that because he has power with God, he will have divine power and authority with men. The name "Israel" can be translated not only as "God strives" but also as "God persists" or as "God perseveres." It is a fact that it was God who had persevered and who, in the end, prevailed and formed a prince of God out of a Jacob. That chosen vessel then had divine power and authority with men. With love and grace, the Almighty and Everlasting God made Himself weak in order that Jacob could "overcome" Him, and become what the Lord intended him to be from the beginning.

Anyone who reads the story of Jacob in the Bible must recognize that the fulfillment of God's purpose for Jacob was entirely due to the persistence and perseverance of God. It was the love of God that would not let Jacob go until he became Israel. Is it not amazing that the one who wrestled with Jacob allowed himself to be overcome, dare we say defeated? And is this not the mystery of Calvary? For when Jesus died, seemingly at the hands of godless men, at the mercy of Satan, in that moment of supreme brokenness and "defeat," He won for us an eternal salvation. It is also highly significant that at the moment Jacob "defeated" the One who wrestled with him, he himself was broken. So it is with the cross of Jesus, for in the moment that He was crucified, we were also crucified with Him.

Jacob even blesses Pharaoh

Jacob came to that place where he had genuine power and authority. This time it was not through manipulation, or shady deals, or through deceit, or his own natural business acumen and shrewdness. It was rather by the wisdom which God gave him and the life of God in him; by the Spirit of God filling him. He became a man who had power with God and with men. He could even bless Pharaoh. It would be impossible to bless a pharaoh if you did not have power with God. Such blessing comes from derived power. Your power with man is derived from your power with God. One wonders why Pharaoh, the most powerful and influential figure of his day, reacted in the way in which he did to Jacob. Clearly, he sensed that this aged man had extraordinary character and power and that he, Pharaoh, could humble himself before Jacob to receive a blessing for himself and for Egypt.

It is a remarkable fact that from the moment Jacob became Israel, he never again sought to manipulate others. He never manipulated his sons, or his grandsons, or Pharaoh, or Joseph. The manner in which they all related to Jacob reveals the power he had with them. The words he used in the blessings of Reuben, Simeon, and Levi reveal this fact. The old Jacob would have sought to control them, even to blackmail them and thus manipulate them (see Gen. 49:3–7). After Jabbok he is a different man.

To be the head, and not the tail

How much all of this teaches us! The Lord intends and purposes that every one of His children should be "the head and not the tail . . . and be above only . . . and not be beneath" (Deut. 28:13). Jacob's latter years are the illustration of this. To put this truth in New Testament terms, He calls us to be overcomers. For example:

> Nay, in all these things we are more than conquerors through him that loved us.
>
> (Rom. 8:37)

Or again,

> and raised us up with him, and made us to sit with him in the
> heavenly places, in Christ Jesus.
>
> (Eph. 2:6)

In experience, sadly, most of us are not seated with Christ in the
heavenlies, nor are we more than conquerors in all the matters
which make up our daily life. Instead of being the head we are
the tail; instead of being above only, we are nearly always
underneath. We do not have power with God, but men and
circumstances have power over us. The world, its atmosphere,
its fashion, and its system, influences us in every way and
determines how we live and how we think. Instead of reigning
with Christ, everything reigns over us. It is our natural strength
and energy that rules us and insures that we are underneath and
not above, that we are the tail and not the head. We know that
our experience should be otherwise, but the reality is altogether
different.

In the church we suffer so much from an "authority complex." We want to be leaders, to be pastors, or elders; even
"apostles." We want to be anything that has some kind of
authority attached to it. It is the natural ambition that is in fallen
mankind. So much in this world is dependent upon title, upon
status, upon degree, upon position, but that is not true authority.
One can have all of that and possess no spiritual authority. Only
when a man is touched at the heart of his being and is broken,
and like Jacob his hip is dislocated, does he have divine authority
within him. He may not feel it, but everybody else knows it. He
has power with God, and thus he has power with men.

True authority: to be a bondslave of all

The Lord Jesus put this whole matter of authority into its
proper place when He said,

Ye know that they who are accounted to rule over the Gentiles lord it over them; and their great ones exercise authority over them. But it is not so among you: but whosoever would become great among you, shall be your minister [a hired servant]; and whosoever would be first among you, shall be servant of all [bondslave of all].

(Mark 10:42–44)

What a deep and costly path Jacob had to walk before he had that kind of authority; when he was no longer the tail but the head, no longer underneath but only above. It was the love of God that persisted and prevailed with Jacob until he became Israel. It is the same undying and persevering love that will not let us go until His work is also done in us.

Chapter 7

None Other than the House of God

And he [Jacob] lighted upon a certain place, and tarried there all night, because the sun was set. And he took one of the stones of the place, and put it under his head, and lay down in that place to sleep. And he dreamed. And, behold, a ladder set up on the earth, and the top of it reached to heaven. And, behold, the angels of God ascending and descending on it. And, behold, the Lord stood above it, and said, I am the Lord, the God of Abraham thy father, and the God of Isaac. The land whereon thou liest, to thee will I give it, and to thy seed.

And Jacob awaked out of his sleep, and he said, Surely the Lord is in this place. And I knew it not. And he was afraid, and said, How dreadful is this place! This is none other than the house of God, and this is the gate of heaven. And Jacob rose up early in the morning, and took the stone that he had put under his head, and set it up for a pillar, and poured oil upon the top of it. And he called the name of that place Beth-el.

(Gen. 28:11–13; 16–19a)

The house of God

Whenever a matter is first introduced in the Word of God, it is of great importance and significance. This is the first time in the Bible that one of its most important themes appears: "the house of God" (Gen. 28:17). That occasion was when the Lord appeared to Jacob in a dream, and he had said, "This is none other than the house of God." Later Jacob builds an altar at that place and calls it "El-beth-el," "God of the house of God" (Gen. 35:7). In fact, earlier, while Jacob was still with Laban, the Lord had appeared to him and said, "I am the God of the house of God" (Gen. 31:13). It is a meaningful title! It is clear that the divine revelation which Jacob received there had a far-reaching and historic significance. Jacob, of course, never built the house of the Lord; and yet his whole life and history was bounded by this matter.

God's house is to do with genuine worship, with true intercession, and with real fellowship and blessing. As we have seen, Jacob was anything but a worshiper, anything but an intercessor, and anything but a blessing. In fact, but for the grace of God, his natural strength of will and energy would frustrate any divine purpose. We would not normally associate the kind of person Jacob was with the house of the Lord. To associate him with the political world, the business world, and the world of human ambition and endeavor would be no problem. Nevertheless, the fact that the Lord for the second time speaks to Jacob about the change of his name from Jacob to Israel, only underlines the importance the Lord attaches to His house and the necessity of being transformed (see Gen. 35:9–15).

In point of fact, as I have already stated, Jacob never built the house of the Lord. We do not even know if he ever visited Jerusalem, which at that time was a Jebusite city. Certainly he never possessed it. When he left his family house and home, in many ways in despair, God spoke to him about *His* house and home. He was away for at least twenty years, in which time God changed him from Jacob into Israel. It has a heavenly significance that he returns to *the very same place* where God originally gave him that revelation. From this we understand that the house of the Lord was one of the most important, if not *the* most important, aspects of God's purpose for Jacob. This matter lies at the heart of God's eternal purpose for mankind, and it is noteworthy that it is with Jacob that the Lord first introduces it.

The Holy Spirit's preparation of history in the Old Testament

All of this can be clearly seen in the fact that the Holy Spirit seemingly repeats the recording of the history of the people of God three times. Firstly, from Genesis to Judges we have the record of the history of the forefathers: Abraham, Isaac, Jacob, Joseph, and Moses, etc.; the actual birth of the nation in Egypt; and its being led by God through the wilderness into the promised land. This is introductory history.

Secondly, we have four books, 1 and 2 Samuel, and 1 and 2 Kings, called in the LXX "the four books of the kingdom," and one small book, Ruth, which is the introduction to that kingdom. The history of God's people is repeated but with a new emphasis. That new emphasis is the divine purpose and aim in choosing Abraham and the forefathers. That purpose was the throne and the kingdom. In these books everything related to God's redeemed people is traced to this matter of the kingdom. The redeemed are to be the head and not the tail, to be only above and not underneath; they are to be the chief of the nations, God's first-born amongst the nations. What the Lord does with them is the key to human history. It is the only kingdom on earth where God reigns practically; and it represents His authority in this world. His throne and His Lordship are to be expressed there. That kingdom is to be a blessing to the whole world, to be the means by which the light of God and the salvation of God should come to the nations; through which the Messiah will be given as the Savior of the world. Therefore, every king is judged by his obedience to the Word of God or lack of it; his faithfulness or unfaithfulness to the Lord. Insofar as they touch the purpose of God, the events in each reign are viewed either negatively or positively. That kingdom is a picture or type of *the* kingdom of God that will finally come in great power and glory.

Thirdly, the same history, it seems, is repeated in 1 and 2 Chronicles, Ezra, Nehemiah, and Esther. One wonders what is the divine purpose in covering the same history twice. It is true that the compiler of 1 and 2 Chronicles reaches back to Adam and, from him, traces the whole of history in the light of God's purpose. The writer of the books of Ezra and Nehemiah take us on to the coming of the Messiah. (It is, in fact, an interesting point that, according to rabbinical tradition, 1 and 2 Chronicles, Ezra, and Nehemiah were written by the same person.) At a superficial reading, 1 and 2 Chronicles seem to be a repetition of 1 and 2 Samuel and 1 and 2 Kings. It has, however, a vital and meaningful significance. It is a reiteration of history but with a new emphasis: that emphasis is the house of God. The divine purpose in choosing Abraham and through him a people, is not only the throne and the kingdom, but also the house of God. Everything is seen in the light of God's dwelling place and whether it is given the priority that God gives to it. Every king is judged by his attitude to the house of the Lord and what he did concerning it. When we come to the books of Ezra and Nehemiah, we discover that this matter of God's dwelling place lies at the heart of the exile, and everything in the exile is judged by its relationship to it, even though the temple was in ruins. All is centered on the rebuilding and the restoration of God's house, and that remnant which would return to accomplish it. When we come to the New Testament we discover both these aspects: the redeemed of God are "kings and priests" (see Rev. 1:6; 5:10). They are both a kingdom and the house of God!

The house of God in the New Testament

In the New Testament, the house of God is presented in a whole number of ways: the church of God, the body of Christ, the household of faith, the bride of Christ, the wife of the Lamb, or the True Vine. Take, for instance, the words of our Lord Jesus,

> upon this rock I will build my church; and the gates of hell shall not prevail against it.
>
> (Matt. 16:18 KJV)

Or the words of the apostle Paul,

> in whom the whole building, being fitted together, is growing into a holy temple in the Lord, in whom you also are being built together into a dwelling of God in the Spirit.
>
> (Eph. 2:21–22 NASB)

Or again, the apostle Peter,

> unto whom coming, a living stone . . . ye also, as living stones, are built up a spiritual house, to be a holy priesthood, to offer up spiritual sacrifices, acceptable to God through Jesus Christ.
>
> (1 Pet. 2:4–5)

God gives a revelation of the house of God to Jacob

In Genesis 28 we have the first mention of this subject. In a vivid dream, God revealed Himself to someone running away because of his stupid sinfulness. We have no record that Jacob repented at that point, although it is clear that he was in despair and exhausted by the circumstances that he had brought upon himself. It is amazing that the Lord gave to Jacob such a vision which not only spanned time, from eternity to eternity, but was the key to the whole purpose of God. The effect on Jacob was dramatic, although not powerful enough to change him into Israel! It is yet another indication of the incredible strength of Jacob's self-life. He said,

How dreadful is this place. This is none other than the house of
God, and this is the gate of heaven.

(v. 17)

As with many other characters in the Bible, Jacob was "undone"
by this revelation. He knew that what the Lord was showing
him was of tremendous significance. He called it "the house of
God" and "the gate of heaven." At the same time he was filled
with dread. It is almost as if he knew intuitively that this would
be the breaking of the old Jacob.

The dream the Lord gave to Jacob

We need to note carefully the different features of this dream
through which God revealed Himself to Jacob. First of all, you
will notice that he saw "a ladder set up on the earth, and the top
of it reached to heaven" (Gen. 28:12). Is that not beautiful? It
was set up on the earth – it did not come down from heaven –
but its top *reached* heaven.

The second feature is that on this ladder the angels of God
were ascending and descending. They were not descending and
ascending. It would be normal for us to imagine that these
angels would be coming out of heaven and down to the earth
and then returning; the opposite, however, was the truth. Were
these the same angels ascending the ladder with requests or
petitions and returning with the answers? This we are not told.
It is clear, however, that there was some kind of vital heavenly
communication and discourse between earth and heaven
centered on the house of God.

The third and even more remarkable feature is that "the LORD
stood above it and said, I am the LORD, the God of Abraham thy
father, and the God of Isaac" (Gen. 28:13a). The Lord stood
above it or toward it. The Hebrew can be translated "toward,"
"unto," "on," or "upon." It is not clear whether it is the ladder
or Jacob that the Lord stood above or toward. What is clear is

that the Lord stationed Himself in such a way that the ladder and the angels were directly related to Him, as also was Jacob.

God and Jacob

Let us seek to clarify our understanding of these features. It is obvious that they are meaningful. We have four matters: God Himself, Jacob himself, the ladder reaching from the earth to heaven, and the angels ascending and descending.

It is very important that we understand that the house of God is first and foremost a matter related to God Himself, to His throne, and to His authority. It is to be the expression of His mind and His heart. The fulfillment of His eternal purpose is centered there. It is the Lord God who has stationed Himself in direct relationship to this ladder, to the angels, and to Jacob.

Secondly, this house is directly related to Jacob. It has something to do with fallen and worthless human beings like Jacob. Such sinners, redeemed and recreated by God's grace, become the home of God in the Spirit, His dwelling place. The word "angel" in Hebrew means "messenger," and the angels' ascending and descending denotes service. Thus we have here a picture of communication, intercourse, interchange, between earth and heaven, and heaven and earth. The house of God is to be this living link.

The church is not some place with pews or seats where we sit in silent or noisy rows and stare at one another or some man at the front. Of course there may be times when we rightly sit in rows and look at somebody teaching or preaching, but essentially that is not the church. The church has a direct relationship to God Himself. It is *His* house, *His* home, *His* dwelling place, and *His* place of rest.

This is how the Lord describes it in Psalm 132:13–16:

> For the LORD hath chosen Zion; he hath desired it for his habitation.

This is my resting-place for ever: Here will I dwell; for I
have desired it.
I will abundantly bless her provision: I will satisfy her poor
with bread.
Her priests also will I clothe with salvation; And her saints
shall shout aloud for joy.

Note: "her poor," "her priests," "her saints": the saved and
redeemed Jacob is the Lord's eternal resting place, His habitation
or home.

The church, then, is the ladder with all its divine activity.
There is service, communication, and intercourse. It is not
merely routine service, a kind of one-way communication in which we never expect an answer. It is the kind of
interchange where we not only speak to God but we hear
God; where we hear Him and obey Him. Would to God that
everything called a church was something like this! If the
church had this kind of character, its impact on the world
would be colossal. It is a fact that every time it has had this
character or regained it, the world has been turned upside
down.

God's ladder

It is interesting to note that when the Lord Jesus spoke to
Nathanael, He had this story in mind.

Nathanael saith unto him, Whence knowest thou me? Jesus
answered and said unto him, Before Philip called thee, when
thou wast under the fig tree, I saw thee. Nathanael answered
him, Rabbi, thou art the Son of God; thou art King of Israel.
Jesus answered and said unto him, Because I said unto thee, I
saw thee underneath the fig tree, believest thou? thou shalt
see greater things than these. And he saith unto him, Verily,
verily, I say unto you, Ye shall see the heaven opened, and

the angels of God ascending and descending upon the Son of man.

(John 1:48–51)

In these words spoken to Nathanael, the Lord Jesus went to the heart of the matter and interpreted the dream given to Jacob. "You shall see the heaven opened and the angels of God ascending and descending upon the Son of Man." The Lord Jesus is the Son of Man, the Messiah, the Son of the Living God. He is God's Ladder, the ladder set up on earth whose top reaches heaven. In Him heaven and earth have been joined. By Him the will of God is to be done on earth as it is in heaven. In Him the kingdom of God has already come in spiritual character, and will yet come physically and publicly in great power and glory. Communication, interchange, and intercourse between earth and heaven are only in and through Him. If, by the grace of God alone, we are in Him, then we begin to understand what the house of God is. It is not only the Lord Jesus but those also whom He has saved. For the Lord Jesus, and those who are in Him, there is an open heaven. Heaven and earth meet and there is divine intercourse. This is the house of God!

We ought also to note that in Jacob's day a ladder was essential in building a house. It seems that we have in the picture of this ladder a divine building program represented. The building of the house of God is not completed; there is much work to be done. Hence the activity of the angelic host, climbing, as we have noted, from the earth to heaven, and back. We should carefully heed the repeated injunction in the New Testament to let all be done toward "building up." It is related to the building of God's house.

Angels ascending and descending

It should be clear from what I have said that these "angels ascending and descending" are a picture of divine activity, of communication between earth and heaven and heaven and earth. Nevertheless, we must not relegate the angels to a form of typology. They are genuine beings. It hardly needs to be stated that the subject of angelic ministry should be approached with great care and balance. It is possible to become sidetracked and to enter dangerous territory where deception and delusion are the rule of the day. Nonetheless, the angels have been sent forth to minister to those who are the heirs of salvation (see Heb. 1:14). This is not a fairy tale but an issue that is real and practical. The ancient Jewish tradition, based on Scripture, is that after the quorum of ten men necessary for divine service has been reached, then the angels of God immediately move into action to help in the spiritual atmosphere. In the unseen, they are to assist the service and ministry of God's people. Many of our hymns refer to this. For example: "Angels, help us to adore Him, ye behold Him face to face."

In the Word of God, it is clear that, in the Unseen, the angels of God are responsible for watching over the purpose of God and the fulfillment of His Word, the work of God, and the people of God. Until we reach the Glory, we shall never know how much we owe to their ministry. The fact remains that there is angelic ministry and service in the present age. That ministry is related to the house of God in a very powerful if unseen manner, and particularly to the building of it. Christ spoke of Himself as the ladder upon which the angels were ascending and descending under an open heaven. Angelic ministry is directly related to the Messiah, and God's purpose for Him.

He shall be for a sanctuary

If we are ever to have a full understanding of what "the house of God" means, we need to recognize the significance of the words of the Lord Jesus:

Jesus answered and said unto them, Destroy this temple, and in three days I will raise it up. The Jews therefore said, Forty and six years was this temple in building, and wilt thou raise it up in three days? But he spake of the temple of his body. When therefore he was raised from the dead, his disciples remembered that he spake this; and they believed the scripture, and the word which Jesus had said.

(John 2:19–22)

The manner in which John records this is important. His gospel is an interpretation rather than a history. The words of the Lord Jesus had an impact on the minds of the disciples at the time in which they heard them, but they had no understanding of their meaning. Later the Holy Spirit gave spiritual understanding to them. It seems clear from that which the apostle Peter wrote in his first letter that Jesus is God's temple; He is the house of the Lord.

In the Old Testament we read:

behold, a virgin shall conceive, and bear a son, and shall call his name Immanuel [God with us].

(Isa. 7:14)

Then Isaiah continues and says:

The LORD of hosts, him shall ye sanctify; and let him be your fear, and let him be your dread. And he shall be for a sanctuary; but for a stone of stumbling and for a rock of offence to both the houses of Israel.

(Isa. 8:13–14a)

"He shall be for a sanctuary." Note carefully that it is not "He shall build a sanctuary" but He, Himself, will be the house of God. For many, this is hard to understand. How can the Lord be the temple of God?

Yet the apostle Paul declares the same truth:

> Jesus Christ himself being the chief corner stone; In whom all
> the building, fitly framed together, groweth unto a holy
> temple in the Lord; In whom ye also are builded together for
> a habitation of God though the Spirit.
>
> (Eph. 2:20–22 KJV)

Carefully note that Paul, by the Spirit of God, states that the
Messiah is the chief cornerstone of the whole building. He does
not, however, want us to understand that Jesus is only the chief
cornerstone and the rest of the building is something else. He
says, *"In whom* [i.e., in Christ] the whole building, fitly framed
together, grows into a holy temple in the Lord; *in whom* [i.e., in
Christ] ye also are built together for a home of God…"
(emphasis added). The Lord Jesus is not only the chief
cornerstone but He is also the foundation, the head of the
corner, and the top-stone. In other words, He is the beginning
and the end of the house of God and if, by the grace of God, we
are in Him, then we have become part of that sanctuary.

So also is Christ

In yet another place the apostle Paul declares:

> For as the body is one, and hath many members, and all the
> members of the body, being many, are one body: so also is
> Christ.
>
> (1 Cor. 12:12)

It is the same tremendous emphasis that the apostle is giving.
He writes, "so also is Christ." Carefully note again that he does
not say, "For as the body is one and has many members … so
also is the body of which Christ is the head," but "so also is
Christ." He equates all the members of the body with Christ.

Christ is the whole. In the same manner in which your head needs your body to express itself, so we have a wonderful picture of Jesus as the Head and we as the body *incorporated* in Him.

This matter is not open to question, as if the apostle has made an ambiguous statement that is nowhere else confirmed in the New Testament. It is in fact confirmed again and again. In the Roman letter, for example, he again writes:

> For even as we have many members in one body, and all the members have not the same office: so we, who are many, are one body in Christ, and severally members one of another.
>
> (Rom. 12:4–5)

Once more carefully note that it is "one body *in* Christ," not "one body *of* Christ." To state that we are the body of Christ is absolutely true, but to state that we are one body in Christ is something even greater.

Head and body

The headship of Christ is, in fact, a subject of vital importance in our understanding of the church. In the New Testament the picture of the head and body is introduced by the Holy Spirit for the first time in the Bible. Sadly, this is not greatly understood amongst Christian believers. All the other pictures of the church are to be discovered in the Old Testament. For example: the temple of God, the house of God, the household of faith, the vine, the olive tree, and the bridegroom and the bride.

Why is this symbol of the head and body introduced? Some believers think of Christ as the head of a government, the head of a hospital, the head of a university or school, or the head of a great commercial organization. The institution or organization is one thing and the head is another. This is not the way the Holy Spirit has introduced the headship of Christ. One has never seen a living headless body, nor has one ever seen a living bodiless head! For life, the head and the body have to be in practical union. To put this matter in a simple way: My name is Lance Lambert. That is the name of my head and also the name of my body. When we meet in the name of Jesus, when we pray in His name, when we act in His name, it is because we, as the church, are joined to Him and share the name of the whole. In other words, the church cannot fulfill her destiny, cannot fulfill the purpose of God, and cannot be that which God intends her essentially to be in this world, if she is alienated or divorced from the head. It thus becomes clear that Satan's supreme objective is, by one means or another, practically to sever the body from the head. The church then becomes an institution, an organization, or a system, like any other in this world.

What is the church?

If you have followed what I have written, it should be clear that the church, the house of God, is not some special building, with either a steeple or a tower; a physical building, either beautiful or ugly; a place where you lose your umbrella or your handbag. It is obvious, of course, that when children of God meet together they will meet in some physical building; but *that* is not the church. Then again, the church is not a matter merely of ministries, of gifts, of elders and deacons, as if that alone constitutes a church. There are, of course, ministries and gifts; there are apostles, prophets, evangelists, shepherds, and teachers; there are elders and deacons. The church is, however, far more than all of that. When our understanding of the church is limited to those matters, we have missed the real meaning of the church in the mind of God.

The house of God is to be the place where the throne of God is being established spiritually. It therefore has much to do with genuine worship in spirit and in truth. It also has much to do with intercession and costly prayer: the travailing prayer of a nucleus of believers who have become living sacrifices. In such ways the Lord fulfills His will and purpose in the place where the house of God is being built. Consider some of the pregnant phrases in the Scriptures we have already noted: "In Him the whole building fitly framed together, grows into a holy temple in the Lord ... In Him you also are built together..." All these phrases – "fitly framed together," "grows into," "built together" – speak of movement and progress. In practical terms they represent a great amount of costly and sometimes painful work by the Spirit of God. Anything less is not the house of the Lord.

In simple reality this means that God, in His mercy, takes people like you and me and saves us, and then places us in the Christ. With Him we become the dwelling place of God, the place of His rest, and His home. Far from being perfect, it is the place where the Spirit of God is at work. It is like a builder's yard, full of mess. Yet it has divine purpose. Something is always happening. There is a being fitly framed together, a growing into a holy temple in the Lord, a being built together as God's home.

Whether we recognize it or not, the Lord takes "Jacobs" like you and me, and with this unpromising material He builds His house. He takes such to be His dwelling place, His home. There He wants to express Himself in power and glory. He wants to save the unsaved, reveal His heart and mind, express His power and His glory, and change every Jacob into an Israel.

Chapter 8

GOD OF THE HOUSE OF GOD

In the last chapter, we considered the dream in which God appeared to Jacob, and its significance. When Jacob awoke, he recognized that God had revealed Himself to him and that, in a direct manner, he was to be involved in the fulfillment of God's purpose. He took the stone that he had used as a pillow, set it up as a testimony, and poured oil upon it. We have therefore three further matters that are full of divine meaning: the necessity of revelation or illumination, the pillar, and the oil poured out upon it.

The Necessity of Revelation and Illumination

When Jacob returned to the land, the Lord commanded him to build an altar where He had first appeared to him: "Arise, go up to Bethel, and dwell there: and make there an altar unto God who appeared unto thee . . ." Jacob called that place "El-beth-el," God of the house of God (see Gen. 35:1, 7). Carefully note one simple but all-important factor: it was a revelation of Himself. Divine revelation, or illumination, is an absolute necessity. It is not enough to have academic knowledge of the things of God. The Spirit of God has to give enlightenment. It is only when such illumination is given to a child of God that the truth dawns upon him or her with *practical* consequence. Until then it is an academic exercise. It remains head-knowledge without any impact upon our lives and behavior.

David wrote,

> For with thee is the fountain of life: In thy light shall we see light.
>
> (Ps. 36:9)

When I write of the necessity of revelation, I am not referring to some kind of "revelation" extra to the Word of God, but I am writing about the illumination of that which He has already revealed in the Scriptures. The Lord Jesus said to Peter,

> Blessed art thou, Simon Bar-Jonah: for flesh and blood hath not revealed it unto thee, but my Father who is in heaven.
>
> (Matt. 16:17)

There was much flesh in Peter, even in his following of the Lord. He even denied the Lord three times. Deeper, however, than Peter's self-manufactured Christianity and service was the revelation which God had given to him concerning the Lord Jesus. It was that revelation of the person of the Lord Jesus, and the God-given faith which sprang from it, that caused him to weep his way back to the Messiah.

The spirit of wisdom and revelation in the knowledge of Him

When Paul wrote his letter to the church at Ephesus, he expressed the burden he had in prayer for them:

> I ... cease not to give thanks for you, making mention of you in my prayers; that the God of our Lord Jesus Christ, the Father of glory, may give unto you a spirit of wisdom and

revelation in the knowledge of him; having the eyes of your
heart enlightened, that ye may know what is the hope of his
calling, what the riches of the glory of his inheritance in the
saints, and what the exceeding greatness of his power . . .

(Eph. 1:15–19)

Apparently the apostle was afraid that his letter might
become mere material for study and discussion, without
practical impact and consequence. Hence his prayer burden,
for there is no alternative to such revelation. No amount of
head-knowledge will ever be a substitute for it. We need the
eyes of our hearts enlightened that we might know what is
the hope of His calling; it is not enough to know *about* the hope
of His calling. When that spirit of wisdom and revelation is
given to a child of God, he or she knows what is the hope, and
life cannot be the same. We are changed by this kind of
knowledge, and it comes only by the illumination which the
Holy Spirit gives.

When God first appeared to Jacob, it was a real revelation,
but it did not touch the heart of the matter in Jacob. There is no
doubt about the effect it had on him, but he was not changed
into Israel by it. The impact on him was so real that he
exclaimed, "Surely the LORD is in this place; and I knew it not."
He went on to describe his feelings, saying, "How dreadful is
this place! This is none other than the house of God, and this
is the gate of heaven." He then set up a pillar of stone, and
poured oil on it, and said,

"If God will be with me, and will keep me in this way that I go,
and will give me bread to eat, and raiment to put on, so that I
come again to my father's house in peace, then shall the LORD
be my God, and this stone, which I have set up for a pillar,
shall be God's house: and of all that thou shalt give me I will
surely give the tenth unto thee."

(Gen. 28:20b–22 mg)

He was, in my estimation, totally unconscious of how superior his words sound. It seems that he felt he was doing God a favor. Incredible as it may seem, he bargained with God as if the Lord was an equal.

God of the house of God

Later when the Lord changed Jacob into Israel at Jabbok, Jacob called that encounter "the face of God." This time the revelation of God broke him and changed him. It seems that there are degrees of revelation, and the Lord knows exactly when to give the illumination that is required. Jacob was clearly not ready at that earlier point for a revelation that would pulverize him and make him a prince with God and with men. The Lord recognized that Jacob would have to pass through many preparatory experiences before he was ready for the revelation that transformed him. After Jabbok He knew that Jacob was ready to return to the land. He had come full circuit, and thus when he came back to the place where the Lord first appeared to him, he built an altar, and called it "God of the House of God." His focus was now on *the person of the Lord* and not himself. There was no bargaining anymore. He saw God's house in relation to the Lord Himself.

The need to see the church as the practical body of Christ

More deeply than I could ever express in words, I believe that we have to see the Lord Jesus with the eyes of our heart, before we "see" the Church. Most of our problems in Christian circles on the subject of the Church have been that we are "seeing" the Church and not seeing the Lord. We understand it in its different denominational patterns and with its manifold organizational problems, whether they are contemporary or

traditional. For many Christians the church is a physical
building, or place, to which you go and from which you leave.
For some, it is an institution, or an organization built,
supported, and managed in much the same way as worldly
establishments and clubs. In the book of Acts, or indeed in the
New Testament as a whole, you will search in vain to find such
a "Church."

Beyond the institutional, organizational, and denominational
systems, the "true Church" is seen by many as the mystical
body of the Lord Jesus. We are told that all born-again believers
belong to that body. We are taught, however, that the body of
Christ is invisible: it is wholly in the Unseen. According to this
concept, we are not meant to see it in action. It is a heavenly
and spiritual entity with little earthly application. It has no
practical impact or influence upon world society; nor is it meant
to have such impact.

Those who understand the Church in this manner make a
dichotomy between the heavenly Church and the Church on
earth. They often make it *in such a manner* that the two have
hardly any practical relationship to one another. The former is
heavenly, eternal, spiritual, and perfect; the latter is earthly,
temporal, imperfect, and sometimes contradictory of the
heavenly!

A pre-Pentecost Church?

There is no doubt that the Word of God clearly teaches that the
Church is expressed on earth and in time by churches: i.e.,
congregations, or assemblies of those who belong to the Lord.
One, however, wonders why the Lord Jesus, before He
ascended to the right hand of the Father, so clearly commanded
His disciples to wait until the Holy Spirit came upon them. By
normally accepted standards, that pre-Pentecost congregation
was a perfect congregation! Was it then only a matter of
spiritual gifts and spiritual power?

The Church after Pentecost, Head and body in practical terms

Before Pentecost the one hundred and twenty believers were united, devoted, had a real experience in prayer, and had no problem with either heresy or liberal theology. Most Christians would be overjoyed with such an assembly! When, however, the Holy Spirit came upon them, the one hundred and twenty units in a congregation became one hundred and twenty members of a body, organically and practically united to its head in heaven. Hearing and obeying the head, the Church became a heavenly powerhouse on earth. The consequence was tremendous. The world was turned upside down, and that without all the paraphernalia we believe today is an absolute necessity for successful evangelism and church building.

When we read the book of Acts, and the New Testament in general, we discover that the Church, the body of our Lord Jesus, is everywhere seen in action, and has such impact that the world is revolutionized. Even social conditions in unsaved society are impacted and changed. Neither the Jewish establishment and hierarchy nor Roman power and authority could withstand it, let alone eradicate it! Moreover, we should note that whenever the Holy Spirit has intervened to recover the real nature of the Church, in successive moves in the last 1,900 years, the world has again been impacted in the same manner.

As I have already stated, there is no substitute for illumination and enlightenment. Revelation is a principle, and without it there can be no building of the house of God. We have to see the Church as *in the Messiah*. We have to see it as "one body *in* Christ"; we have to see the head and body as one whole. Simply stated, this means the Church has its head at the right hand of God, and the Holy Spirit makes this union a reality in practical terms. "He is the head of the body, the church," not the figurehead (see Col. 1:18)! Where there is no living experience of the Holy Spirit, no illumination or revelation of the Lord

Jesus, Christians have fallen back on the "arm of the flesh" and have produced systems, routines, and methodologies of various kinds. There is nothing wrong with method, with routine, or organization until they become the substitute for the real thing. Instead of a humble dependence upon the Lord, we have "systems," organization, and methodology. Once that has taken place, the church routine can rumble on, with all its meetings, whether the Lord is there or not. Christ is no longer the actual and practical head: He has become a mere figure-head! The living, functioning union between the head and the body has been severed.

Sadly, the history of the Church in the last millennia has given ample evidence for this. Every recovery move of the Holy Spirit has, within a few generations, degenerated in this manner. The building work of the Lord Jesus has ceased, and something else has taken over. Only when the Messiah Jesus is given the place the Father has given to Him, will the building work continue. Otherwise, what was once His work becomes a façade; it has the look of the real thing, but it is not His work. The scaffolding remains, but the building has ceased!

Faithful to "church truth"

There are other precious believers who seek to be faithful in this matter of the "New Testament Church," and who seek to restore it and build it. For such, "church truth" is all important. If, however, it is "truth" academically understood, as quickly as they have gathered together, so quickly they break up and disappear. They became excited and stirred up by certain truths which they observed in the Word of God and began to meet together, not on the foundation of Christ, but on the "truth of the Church." Such companies frequently turn inwards, slowly stagnate, and die. Often they become the platform for petty dictatorships. It is well that we should remember the words of the Psalmist:

Except the LORD build the house, They labor in vain that build it . . .

(Ps. 127:1)

How is it possible that those who recognize church truth and who faithfully seek to express it, end with something so far from the reality of the Church? The answer is that it was head knowledge and not the revelation of the Lord. The key is whether we see the Church in Christ, or whether we see it as a truth detached from Him.

As I have stated a number of times, revelation is a divine principle, and without it there can be no building of the house of God. Have you seen with the eyes of your heart the Church in terms of seeing the Lord? If you have, you will be able to understand why Jacob called that place of revelation "God of the House of God."

First Love: the missing element

One must, however, make one further point. There are Christians who have had genuine revelation concerning the Church; they have seen the Church in Christ, and gathered together on that foundation. Yet, those gatherings have also disappeared. The reason for it is simple. Like Jacob, the revelation which they received did not break them. The truth began to be manipulated and exploited for personal ends. Authority, ministry, and gifts became all important. The Church became the sphere for building an empire, either large or small. The missing element was first love for the Lord Jesus.

It is of supreme importance that we recognize the practical truth which the apostle Paul expressed in the thirteenth chapter of his first letter to the Corinthians. That chapter is often torn out of its context and made to stand on its own. Indeed, it can stand on its own! It is, however, placed in one of the most practical expositions in the New Testament concerning the body of the Messiah. Paul has already spoken of the Lord's table and the body of Christ in chapters 11 and 12, and continues to write about the meetings of the church in chapter 14. He introduces chapter 13 with the words, "And moreover a most excellent way show I unto you" (12:31), and ends with the words, "Let love be your greatest aim" (14:1 LB).

This kind of love is born in us when God reveals His face to us; when the light of the knowledge of the glory of God in the face of Jesus shines into us, and changes us. It is the Holy Spirit at work through the cross, breaking our self-life and filling us with divine love.

At the heart of true church building there has to be always a nucleus of believers who are living sacrifices, their lives laid down for the love of Christ. And even more, they have to remain "in love" with Him. That love for Him is the power of our love for one another. This is the quality of first love. The house of the Lord is built up not by mere knowledge but by such love.

Knowledge can be accumulated from books and from good and serious study. There is nothing wrong in the genuine study of God's Word. However, without illumination and enlightenment, our knowledge can make us proud, arrogant, and self-sufficient. We can take a superior position to others. Even worse, we can exploit the church and the work of God for our own ends. Such an attitude is loveless. All the seeds of faction, division, rivalry, jealousy, and "empire-building" are found here. "Knowledge puffeth up, but love edifieth" (1 Cor. 8:1). No wonder the Holy Spirit says, "Make love your aim."

The Pillar

Jacob ... took the stone that he had put under his head, and set it up for a pillar, and poured oil upon the top of it. And he called the name of that place Beth-el.

(Gen. 28:18–19)

This is the second matter that is full of divine meaning and significance. In Hebrew the word translated in English as "pillar" is a memorial stone or pillar. It is clear that when such a stone was set up in the time of the Old Testament, it was as a witness (e.g. Gen. 31:44–52; cf. Josh. 24:21–27). In this instance when Jacob set up the stone, which he had used originally as a pillow, it was as a testimony to a meeting with God. God gave him a revelation of Himself, the significance of which can never be overemphasized. At that point in Jacob's life he would not have fully understood its meaning, but he called that place *Beth-el*, the house of God. The fact that this event is mentioned a number of times in the story of Jacob reveals the importance which the Holy Spirit attaches to it (Gen. 28:19, 22; 31:13; 35:15).

The church: a witness and a testimony

The house of the Lord is not only to be a place of genuine worship and intercession, but supremely it is to be a witness and a testimony to both the unseen and seen worlds. When it loses this vital aspect of its constitution and calling, it loses its true meaning. It then becomes an outward form with a mechanically performed routine. The apostle Paul refers to this essential calling of the church when he wrote,

> to the intent that now unto the principalities and the powers in the heavenly places might be made known through the church the manifold wisdom of God.

> (Eph. 3:10)

The church on earth is to be the expression of the Lord Jesus in the unseen, invisible world. This is part of the calling of the church.

The church holding the testimony of Jesus

In his first letter to Timothy, Paul wrote:

> but if I tarry long, that thou mayest know how men ought to
> behave themselves in the house of God, which is the church of
> the living God, the pillar and ground of the truth.
>
> (1 Tim. 3:15)

He refers to the church of God as "the pillar and ground of
the truth." It is clear to me that, in using the term "pillar," the
apostle saw the church as holding the testimony of Jesus. He
saw the calling of the church to be a living witness to the Lord
Jesus. The Messiah Himself had said to His disciples just before
His ascension, "Ye shall be witnesses unto me." Paul's burden
for Timothy was that he should understand that this was not
merely doctrinal but was to govern all conduct and behavior.
"That you may know how men ought to behave themselves in
the house of God." From the greatest apostle to the humblest
saint, from the conduct of the meetings to the character of
the family, from the corporate to the personal, all was to be
governed by this matter.

Sound doctrine is essential, and its importance must never be
devalued or understated. It is a vital part of "holding the
testimony of Jesus." Nevertheless, our conduct and behavior
needs to match the truths we proclaim. The apostle Paul in his
last letter to Timothy wrote:

> All Scripture is inspired by God and profitable for teaching, for
> reproof, for correction, for training in righteousness . . .
>
> (2 Tim. 3:16 NASB)

It is noteworthy that Paul emphasizes the intensely practical
result of God's Word even more when he writes: "that the man
of God may be adequate, equipped for every good work"
(v. 17).

When the tabernacle was first set up as the house of the Lord,
it was called "the Tabernacle of the Testimony" (Exod. 38:21).
Every piece of furniture in it was part of this testimony, from

the tablets of stone upon which the Ten Commandments were written, to the tent of meeting, from the Ark of the Covenant, to the altar of burnt offering, and the laver. The writer of the Hebrew letter spoke of all these things as a "copy and shadow of the heavenly things." It mattered not where you stood in the tabernacle or the temple: everything spoke of the Lord. It was a testimony to Him and a witness of Him. It is no wonder that the psalmist declared, "And in his temple everything saith, Glory" (Ps. 29:9). From the colors used to the weaving of the veil, from the woodwork to the gold and to the silver used, everything expressed the beauty and the glory of the Lord. What a wonderful picture this is of the calling of the church to be the testimony of Him in the earth. She is to be the expression of His saving power and majestic glory, both in the seen and the unseen world.

The golden lampstand gives light

It is interesting to note that as you progress in the Bible, you discover that it is the golden lampstand that is chosen to represent the whole tabernacle and temple. To Zechariah it was revealed that this signified an essential building program concerning the house of the Lord, and to which every ministry was related (see Zech. 4). Likewise, the Lord Jesus reveals to the apostle John that each of the seven churches, expressing the Church on earth and in time, is represented by a golden lampstand. It is obvious that the principal use of a lampstand is to give light, and thus it symbolizes testimony and witness (see Rev. 2 and 3).

The church routine rumbling on without the testimony of Jesus

When the Lord Jesus, speaking to the church in Ephesus, warns them that He will remove their lampstand out of its place, we come to the heart of the matter. It is perfectly clear that the church in Ephesus would continue with its prayer meetings, its Bible studies, its evangelistic meetings, and the Lord's Table. What then would be removed, and what is it that they would lose? Whatever it was that the removal of the lampstand represented, and whatever constituted the loss, it is apparent that many would not have noticed its removal, or felt its loss!

This is even more clear when we come to the church in Laodicea. Here is a church which believed it had "arrived" and was in need of nothing. It believed it was spiritually rich and wealthy, whereas the Lord described its real condition as "wretched ... miserable ... poor ... blind ... and naked." They met in the name of the Lord, remembered Him in the breaking of bread, studied His word, preached His gospel, and *He* was outside of the assembly. He was knocking on the door from the outside. Unmistakably the church in Laodicea had suffered loss, and yet the majority of the believers, including its leadership, were unaware of it.

For the Head of the church to be outside of it, His voice unheard, is surely total loss! It is amazing to hear the Lord saying to those whom He has saved, and who belong to Him, "if any man hear my voice and open the door ... " (Rev. 3:20). The fact is that the lampstand was in serious danger of being removed, if it had not already been removed. They would then no longer hold the testimony of Jesus, although the church routine would rumble on.

How many times has this tragedy been re-enacted in the history of the Church? Unknowingly, unseen, the testimony of Jesus has been withdrawn; and it all began with a loss of first-love. Whole powerful movements of the Spirit of God have died. They have crystallized, become institutionalized, and have been denominationalized: they have become a monument to past experience of the power and the glory of God. It is also true of many assemblies and works of God. Where once the Spirit of God worked in amazing ways, people were saved, believers were built up, and there was such a sense of the Lord's presence and power; there is now only death, and at the best only the ashes of that which was once the fire of God.

I am the light of the world: ye are the light of the world

What is this testimony and witness that is represented by the golden lampstand, if it is not the testimony of Jesus? We find this phrase in a number of places in the New Testament (e.g., Rev. 1:2, 9; 19:10; cf. 1 Cor. 1:6; 2 Tim. 1:8). It is interesting to note that John writes of "holding the testimony of Jesus," in the manner in which the golden lampstand held the lamps. Essentially this testimony is not ours, it is His; we hold it. He spoke of Himself as the light of the world:

> I am the light of the world: he that followeth me shall not walk in the darkness but shall have the light of life.
>
> (John 8:12)

Note carefully that it is the light of *life* and not the light of knowledge. This kind of enlightenment comes from His life within us and is always the work of the Holy Spirit illuminating God's Word, and applying it to us and to our circumstances.

It is important to note that the Lord Jesus not only spoke of Himself as the light of the world but also declared that those whom He saved were to be the light of the world (Matt. 5:14). He uses the exact same description of us as of Himself. The meaning is clear: the Lord in us is the light! It is in this union between Himself and those whom He saves, that we discover the house of the Lord.

The house of God is not there for me and for my fulfillment. First and foremost it is there for Him. It is His dwelling place, His home in the Spirit. It is concerned with His fulfillment, His destiny, and His glory. Who is destined for the throne? The Lord Jesus! Upon whom shall all the glory and power rest? The Lord Jesus! Who is the heir of all things? The Lord Jesus! The wonder of it all is that He has saved us and is determined to share His glory, His throne, and His destiny with us.

The only way that sinners could ever inherit the kingdom of God is through that which the Lord Jesus accomplished at Calvary. The tabernacle and the temple had another side to them that I have not mentioned. They were places full of blood and death. All those sacrifices speak of the Lord Jesus. They too were a testimony and a witness. By the sacrifice of Himself alone could He bring many sons to glory and make them heirs of God with Himself.

Before we leave this matter of "the Pillar," there is another facet of its meaning. The Lord Jesus, as I have already mentioned, said to His disciples, "ye shall be my witnesses . . ." (Acts 1:8 or KJV, "ye shall be witnesses unto me"). Witnessing, by its inherent nature, cannot be second-hand. To be a witness one has to have a direct, personal, first-hand involvement in the matter at hand. You have to be an eyewitness. Every member of the body of our Lord Jesus ought to have his or her own ongoing experience of Him. The church of God, in its every aspect, has to be alive with His life, if it is to hold the testimony of Jesus. There has to be first-hand experience, not second-hand or third-hand. Its meetings should be alive with His presence and should be times in which God speaks and God works.

The Oil

> And Jacob rose up early in the morning, and took the stone which he had put under his head, and set it up for a pillar, and poured oil upon the top of it. And he called the name of that place Beth-el.
>
> (Gen. 28:18–19a)

Jacob poured oil upon the pillar. Anyone who knows their Bible will know that, throughout its pages, oil is a symbol of the person and work of the Holy Spirit. Here, in this event, we have another example that has been written for our instruction. In one sense, it seems an odd thing to pour oil on a stone. It has, however, vital meaning. When Jacob returned to the land, he again set up a pillar in the same place and again poured oil upon it (Gen. 35:14). It is also highly instructive that when the Lord appeared to Jacob at the end of the twenty years he had spent with his uncle Laban, the Lord said:

> I am the God of Beth-el where thou anointedst a pillar, where thou vowedst a vow unto me: now arise, get thee out from this land, and return unto the land of thy nativity.
>
> (Gen. 31:13)

The Lord emphasized the fact that Jacob had poured oil upon the pillar. He described it as "anointing" it.

Without the person and work of the Holy Spirit, there is no house of God

Here we discover the third matter that is full of divine meaning. There is no way the house of God can be built without the person and work of the Holy Spirit. It is impossible to hold the testimony of Jesus, or to see the divine purpose realized in our day and generation, without the Holy Spirit. When Jacob anointed the pillar with oil, whether he fully understood it or not, it was a declaration that he could never be transformed into Israel apart from the Holy Spirit. It was also a declaration that the house of God could not be built unless the Spirit of God was in charge.

Many years later, the Lord gave the prophet Zechariah a vision of the temple's seven-branched golden lampstand. I have already drawn attention to this fact. The Lord was speaking about the rebuilding of the house of God, and said it would be rebuilt and completed "not by might, nor by power, but by My Spirit" (Zech. 4:6). Insurmountable problems and difficulties faced the people of God at that time. Those problems and difficulties constituted an enormous and immovable mountain, and the people were confused, depressed, and paralyzed. Then the Lord spoke,

> Who art thou, O great mountain? before Zerubbabel thou shalt become a plain; and he shall bring forth the top stone with shoutings of Grace, grace, unto it. Moreover the word of the LORD came unto me, saying, The hands of Zerubbabel have laid the foundation of this house; his hands shall also finish it; and thou shalt know that the LORD of hosts hath sent me unto you.
>
> (Zech. 4:7–9)

It was all to be accomplished not by human ingenuity or power but by the Spirit of God.

The problem that many believers have, is that they think of the Holy Spirit as a power, an agency, or an instrument: an "it." For them He is not a person. However, the Word of God commands us,

> grieve not the Holy Spirit of God, in whom ye were sealed unto the day of redemption.
>
> (Eph. 4:30)

You cannot grieve an influence or an instrument. The Holy Spirit is a person, and it is a wonderful day when a child of God for the first time recognizes that fact.

Since the Holy Spirit never draws attention to Himself but always to the Lord Jesus, it is possible to ignore the essential nature of His work. Nevertheless, if we devalue or ignore the person and the work of the Holy Spirit, it will be at our peril and loss.

Without the Holy Spirit there is no practical experience of Christ

It is a fact that we will never know true repentance, or a genuine conviction of sin, or the reality of a new-birth apart from the Holy Spirit. All of that is His essential work. Furthermore, we cannot grow in the Lord, or be changed into His likeness, or be gifted, empowered, or equipped for service, without the Holy Spirit. Indeed, without Him there is nothing. He enables us to walk with the Lord Jesus and to hear Him. It is His work to turn our eyes upon Jesus; to make real to us, and in us, that which the Messiah accomplished in His finished work. It is impossible to fulfill a divine calling or ministry, or to work the work of God, without the Holy Spirit.

When the Lord Jesus said, "ye shall be my witnesses," He prefaced those words with, "ye shall receive power, when the Holy Spirit is come upon you" (Acts 1:8). That in itself gives us the clue as to how essential and vitally necessary is the person and the work of the Holy Spirit. You cannot be an effective and loving witness of the Lord Jesus without the Holy Spirit coming upon you. You remain a hard, inanimate and cold stone! That stone needs oil poured upon it.

The Holy Spirit and the last phase of world history

Many years ago I remember Theodore Austin-Sparks[2] recounting to me that, when he was a young man, he went to see A.B. Simpson[3] and asked him what he thought would be the

2. Theodore Austin-Sparks (1888–1971) was one of the genuine prophetic voices of the twentieth century in the Church of God. He was greatly contradicted and withstood by many Christian leaders. In the life and ministry of Watchman Nee he had, however, a very real influence.
3. A.B. Simpson (1843–1919) was the founder of the Christian and Missionary Alliance. He was one of the greatest voices in North America and had a worldwide influence in the latter part of the nineteenth century and the first half of the twentieth century. A.W. Tozer was his spiritual successor.

main characteristic of God's work in the last phase of world history. A.B. Simpson thought for a while and said, "It will be characterized by a new discovery of the person and work of the Holy Spirit on the part of God's people." I asked Mr Sparks what he thought about A.B. Simpson's answer, and he said, "Nothing else will ever carry the people of God through the last part of world history, unless they rediscover the real power of the Holy Spirit."

There may have been many excesses and failings in what is popularly called the "Charismatic Revival," but there can be little doubt that millions have come to know the Lord through it; or that many more believers were brought back to their first-love, rediscovered their Bibles, and became living and powerful witnesses to the Lord Jesus. Since it is the Holy Spirit who practically supervises the fulfillment of both the purpose and work of God, it would seem strange if there were no further, and even more powerful, movements of God's Spirit in whatever time is left. If the work of God is to be completed, the house of God to be finished, and the bride made ready, the Lord will need continuously to realign and re-empower those who would be faithful to Him. The only key to all of this is the person and work of the Holy Spirit.

The cost of being fully committed

The whole history of the Church is filled with examples of those who "stoned the prophets," and a few generations later built their sepulchers and cherished their memory. For example, take Martin Luther. In his day it cost much to be in any way associated with that servant of God, called by some "the drunken monk." His "new-fangled" doctrines of justification by faith, and the supremacy and authority of God's Word were considered by many believers to be radical and overboard! A century later he was hailed as the great reformer, and the truths he preached as foundational. Another example was John Wesley, who in his day was looked upon by many as a dissident and wild preacher, and was turned out of many pulpits. They called him and those associated with him "Enthusiasts." His emphasis on the necessity of a new birth was considered to be another "new-fangled" doctrine. Within a generation he was revered, even in the Church of England out of which he was cast, and the truth he preached was recognized as fundamental to the gospel. One could mention so many more examples. It costs to be part of what God is doing in one's own day and generation.

The essential nature of the anointing of the Holy Spirit

It is worth emphasizing that when the Lord Himself referred to Jacob pouring oil on the pillar he had set up, He described it as *anointing* the pillar. Wherever you look in the Word of God, you will discover that whoever and whatever God uses has to be anointed. The prophet, the priest, and the king had to be anointed; everything in the tabernacle, from the tent of meeting to the furniture and to the holy vessels, also had to be anointed. In other words, anointing was essential to everyone and everything that God called and desired to use.

The Lord Jesus poured out the promised Holy Spirit on the Day of Pentecost, and from that day forward the empowering and the indwelling of the Holy Spirit is a fundamental necessity for every child of God. Some Christians put all the emphasis on the indwelling of the Holy Spirit, whilst ignoring the empowering of the Holy Spirit. Others put all the emphasis on the empowering of the Holy Spirit. However, both aspects of His work are essential for the individual believer, for those who would serve the Lord, and for the building and completion of the house of God.

The pillar and the altar

It is also noteworthy that when Jacob returned to the exact place in the land where the Lord had appeared to him at first, he not only anointed the pillar again but he built there an altar (see Gen. 35:1, 3, 7). In the Bible, the altar is always a type and picture of the cross. In the same way that there are two vital aspects of the Holy Spirit's work, His indwelling and His empowering, so there are two vital aspects of the work of the Lord Jesus at Calvary. He died *for* me and He died *as* me. Both these aspects are found in the statement of the apostle Paul:

> I have been crucified with Christ; and it is no longer I that live, but Christ liveth in me: and that life which I now live in the flesh I live in faith, the faith which is in the Son of God, who loved me, and gave himself up for me.
>
> (Gal. 2:20)

It is impossible for the purpose of God to be realized or completed without the work of the cross. One cannot divorce the work of the Holy Spirit from the work of the cross. We are not told whether Jacob used the pillar he anointed as the altar stone, but it makes no difference to the truth. We need both the full work of the Holy Spirit, and the full work of the cross, in the life and service of the church and in our lives as individual believers, if God's purpose is ever to be fulfilled.

Chapter 9

I HAVE SEEN GOD
FACE TO FACE

When we come to the story of Jacob at Jabbok, we have come to the heart of the matter. There is no doubt that what happened to him at Jabbok was the most notable event in his life and destiny. This is the first time the name "Israel" appears in the divine record. That fact alone makes this meeting between the Lord and Jacob eternally significant. In words that are both striking and meaningful, Isaiah declares that the Lord created Jacob, and through His redeeming work and power alone, out of Jacob formed Israel (Isa. 43:1). It is a revelation of the grace of God when He declares, "I have called you by your name." That name is both "Jacob" and "Israel." It is not possible to have an *Israel* without first a *Jacob*. Here then is the heart of the matter.

In the account of what happened to Jacob at Jabbok, there is a delightful play on words in the Hebrew, and it cannot be a coincidence. You have "Jabbok," *yaboq*, Jacob, *ya'aqob*, and to "wrestle," *ye'abeq* (see Gen. 32:22–24). These are the three constituents in the story: Jabbok the place, Jacob the twister, and the wrestling of the Lord and Jacob.

Jabbok the place

Jabbok is the name of a small seasonal river that has its source near Amman and flows some 65 miles or 96 kilometers through

a wild and deep ravine into the river Jordan. It is today called
Wadi Zerka. Jacob and his family crossed it at a ford which
forever afterwards was called *Penuel*. *Penuel*, or *Peniel*, means
"face of God" or "presence of God." The Hebrew idea is that
the face reveals and expresses the person. Your face is your
presence!

We have this same word in the Aaronic priestly blessing:

> The LORD bless thee, and keep thee: the LORD make his face to
> shine upon thee, and be gracious unto thee: the LORD lift up his
> countenance upon thee, and give thee peace.
>
> (Num. 6:24–26)

Both the words in English, "face" and "countenance," are the
Hebrew word *pan*, the face or the presence of the Lord.

Another example is when the Lord said to Moses, "My
presence shall go with thee, and I will give thee rest"; and Moses
said, "If thy *presence* go not with me, carry us not up hence"
(Exod. 33:14–15, emphasis added). It is the same word. It would
sound awkward in English to say, "My face will go with you
and I will give you rest." The fact that in the Hebrew "with
you" and "with me" are not in the original text makes this
matter even more clear. The literal translation would be, "My
presence will go, and I will give you rest," but that would also
sound awkward in English. We could deduce from the normal
translation that the Lord would support us and back us in *our*
endeavors. The true meaning, however, is that when the Lord
moves, we move with His presence, and find both rest and
power in the fulfilling of *His* work and purpose.

Jacob the twister

When Jacob later described this encounter with God the
deepest experience of his whole life, he called it "the face of
God." He could have called it "brokenness" or "devastation":

it would have been an apt description of what happened to him at Jabbok. He was utterly broken and devastated, his hip being so dislocated that for the rest of his life he limped. He could therefore rightly have called it "lameness," but he did not. If he had wanted to be more positive, he could have called it "conversion" or "transformation": it would have been true. He could have described it as "blessing," "a second blessing," "a baptism of the Spirit," and again it would have been a good description. The fact that he called it "the face of God" or "the presence of God" reveals that he had become Christ-centered. What happened to Jacob at Jabbok was swallowed up by his sense that it was the presence of the Lord, the shining of the face of God upon him. It was as if the light of the knowledge of the glory of God in the face of Jesus the Messiah had shone upon him and into him, both breaking him and making him. It was not the brokenness that gripped him: it was the presence of the Lord. That experience of the Lord changed him forever. For the first time Jacob saw himself as he really was, and out of that experience he emerged as Israel.

Jacob said, "I have seen God face to face, and my life is preserved." His testimony is the more remarkable in the light of what the Lord Jesus Himself said,

> Blessed are the pure in heart: for they shall see God.
>
> (Matt. 5:8)

Most people would never have considered that Jacob was a candidate for seeing God. Indeed, the statement of the Lord Jesus would seem to rule out a person like Jacob. What then did the Lord mean by the phrase "the *pure* in heart"? Was there something in Jacob, deeper than his guile and shrewd acumen, a longing for God, a desire for the Lord, which God recognized as a "purity of heart"? Certainly there was in Jacob a recognition of the value of eternal things, a consuming desire for the Lord. It was for that reason that he wanted the birthright and the blessing. The Spirit of God took hold of that deep longing for God in Jacob, which only the Lord could see. God had so dealt with Jacob that, when Jacob's opportunity came, he gripped the heavenly visitor in a night-long wrestling clinch, and would not let him go.

The wrestling of the Lord and Jacob

How noteworthy is the account in Genesis 32:24: "And Jacob was left alone; and there wrestled a man with him until the breaking of the day." Who was this heavenly visitor? When Hosea recounts this event, he records that Jacob "had power over the angel, and prevailed; he wept, and made supplication unto him: he found him at Beth-el, and there he spake with us, even the LORD, the God of hosts; the LORD is his memorial [name]" (Hos. 12:4–5).

Although he does not speak of the angel as the "Angel of the Lord" or "the Angel of His presence," he seems to equate him with the LORD. Carefully note that "he found *him* at Beth-el." Compare this with Genesis 28:12–13. It seems reasonable to understand this was the Lord Himself. It is striking that the account in Genesis describes this heavenly visitor as a man. Is this not the Lord Jesus? The work of the Lord Jesus at Calvary underlies the whole of history, and has always been the only way in which God has turned "Jacobs" into "Israels." There is no other possibility! Was this a pre-incarnation appearance of the Messiah? If it was the Messiah, He surely had the power to defeat Jacob. It would seem that He did not use His full power, but instead allowed Himself to be defeated!

Jabbok and Calvary

The Bible is full of types and figures, nearly all of which are centered in the finished work of the Messiah on the cross. The apostle Paul wrote,

Now these things happened unto them by way of example; and they were written for our admonition, upon whom the ends of the ages are come.

(1 Cor. 10:11)

The Greek word translated "by way of example" is also the word for "type" or "figure." It could be translated, "These things happened to them as types..." Jabbok is one of those types. In many ways it is a perfect picture of Calvary, a prophetic enactment of something that was to be fulfilled thousands of years ahead.

Here, in what happened at Jabbok, is a picture, or figure, of the Son of God, crucified through weakness, and in that weakness displaying absolute and total power to save and change a sinner into His own likeness. Calvary is truly the face of God, for there we see what God is like. On the cross, in the crucified Messiah, God revealed Himself. There we see His mind and His heart expressed. At no point in the whole of history has the presence of God been more manifest than when Jesus was crucified. Through that finished work of the Messiah Jesus, the power of God was released to save to the uttermost those who will come to God by Him. It is no wonder that Paul proclaimed,

we preach Christ crucified; unto Jews a stumblingblock, and unto Gentiles foolishness; but unto them that are called, both Jews and Greeks, Christ the power of God, and the wisdom of God.

(1 Cor. 1:23–24)

On the cross, the One who is the Almighty, allowed Himself to be defeated that He might save and transform. It is there that God reveals His face.

When the Lord Jesus was crucified, He died for us and at the same time He died as us. To quote the apostle Paul yet again,

> I have been crucified with Christ; and it is no longer I that live,
> but Christ living in me: and that life which I now live in the
> flesh I live in faith, the faith which is in the Son of God, who
> loved me, and gave himself up for me.
>
> (Gal. 2:20)

We can be saved from our sins, but the problem of our self-life,
the sin principle, remains. We can still be egocentric; we can be
self-serving, self-fulfilling, and self-glorying. When the Lord
Jesus died at Calvary, it was a full salvation that He wrought.
He was made sin for us; He took our place and died for our sin.
Therefore, we can testify, "He loved me, and gave Himself *for*
me." At the same time, He died *as* us. We were crucified *with*
Him that we might be delivered from a self-centered, self-
fulfilling, and self-assertive life. This is the powerful truth which
Jabbok expresses. It is a type or figure of Calvary.

Lessons from Jabbok

The necessity of Jabbok

It is clear that Jabbok was a necessity if the purpose of God for
Jacob was to be fulfilled. In principle every true believer must
experience what Jacob experienced there. In no other way
could Jacob become Israel. There was, and is, no alternative
to Jabbok. Jacob's natural character, his talented self-life, his
amazing natural resilience insured that no previous experience
could change him. Indeed, when the Lord appeared to him at
Bethel, Jacob was left untouched. He even spoke of it as being
"a dreadful place and none other than the house of God ...
and the gate of heaven." He must have sensed that this would
be the end of his self-life, but at that point it left him the same
old Jacob. Indeed, he even bargained with God. Only the kind
of experience that Jacob had at Jabbok pulverized him. There,
in seeing the Lord, he was changed into Israel.

Every servant of the Lord, sooner or later, must come to his or her "Jabbok." We may have had many experiences of the Lord, as indeed Jacob had, but only Jabbok will change us, as it changed him. The Lord may have granted us much illumination but, important as that may be, it can still leave us basically unchanged. It has not reached down to the root of the matter in our life and our service. By the Spirit of God we can see something in the Word of God, and what we see thrills us, excites us, and fills us with wonder. Indeed, such understanding can give direction to our lives, but at the same time does not touch the essential problem. The problem we all have is our self-life. An unbroken self-life will always be *the* obstacle to the full work of the Holy Spirit.

The study of the Word of God is all-important. The more we study His Word and memorize it, the more material there is for the Holy Spirit to work upon. Let us, however, never imagine that the accumulation of knowledge, or the memorizing of Scripture, or even the recognition of spiritual principles, is *in itself* life transforming. Ten years in a theological seminary will never accomplish what one night at Jabbok can accomplish. If you want to be a prince with God, if you want to have power with God and with men, if you want to be an overcomer, if you want to become a blessing to others, a builder of the house of God, there is no alternative to Jabbok.

God's timing of Jabbok

You cannot arrange your "Jabbok" anymore than Jacob could have arranged it. God's timing of it is always perfect. It is never too early and never too late. The Lord works ceaselessly, and normally in hidden ways, to arrange your circumstances, your situations, your relationships, and your problems. At the exact moment in which you have come to a true self-despair, He times your "Jabbok." He is never late in His appointment. Sometimes we want to pressure Him into bringing it forward, but He alone knows when we are ready. It took twenty years with Jacob, and at the beginning of that time he had absolutely no idea about himself. At the end of those years, the Lord's appointed time for Jacob had come. By circumstances, situations, and, above all, relationships, the Lord had well prepared Jacob for Jabbok.

He had told Jacob to return to his homeland, and by so doing had catapulted him into the impossible. There was no way for Jacob and his family to return to the promised land and avoid Esau. It was divine psychology that now brought together self-despair and fear of the future. The Lord had finally cornered him! The divine strategy, as always, was well prepared. Jacob could not pass over this river anywhere, for the Jabbok is a steep gorged river and he had to come to one of its fords. Behind him was Laban and his men, and in front of him was Esau with some four hundred men. Jacob was terrified. Here, at the ford, was this strong, intelligent, shrewd business manipulator; and in this situation he was helpless. He could not talk himself out of this problem. Even so, the old Jacob planned to "soften" Esau by a whole number of gifts. They were to be given on the same day, at small intervals of time, to heighten the effect. Jacob, however, knew that his situation was impossible, and his sense of guilt only made him feel the worse.

The fact that the record says, "the angels of God met him" (Gen. 32:1), is evidence of the divine strategy. Jacob even called that place *Mahanaim*, which means "two companies" or "two encampments." Apparently there were two encampments of angels. Only the Lord could have ordered this. One would have thought that the appearance of the angels would have had a comforting effect on Jacob, calming him and at the same time re-energizing him. It did not. The Lord had done such a good job that Jacob had lost his self-confidence.

Jacob had described them as "God's host," or camp. In his enormous distress and fear of Esau's intention, he then divided his family into two companies. He was probably unsure as to whether the Lord had provided the angels for the protection of his family, or whether they were there to supervise justice being meted out on him for his wrongdoing. His past had now caught up with him. The timing of the Lord, as always, was perfect. Jacob was ready for the greatest experience of his life.

God's timing of your personal "Jabbok," as with Jacob, is always perfect. It may not be as dramatic as Jacob's experience, but the principle is the same. Jabbok is a necessity, and if we are to reach the point that God wants us to reach, it is unavoidable. If we settle for something less, as indeed Jacob could have done by staying with his uncle Laban for the rest of his life, Jabbok could have been avoided. If, however, he was to obey God's command to return to the land, he could not avoid it. We should note that Jacob was bent on obedience, which speaks volumes about his heart! However, that path of obedience led through Jabbok. There God's purpose to change Jacob into Israel was to be fulfilled.

Jacob was left alone

The words "And Jacob was left alone" are striking and poignant (Gen. 32:24). They reveal a divine loneliness which is absolutely essential in this experience. No one can share this with you. Your dearest and most understanding friends cannot be with you; neither your husband, nor your wife, nor your children, nor your parents can be present. You have to be *alone* with the Lord. Even those who have spiritually meant the most to you cannot enter and share this experience with you. By its very nature the Lord separates us from all others, so that we are alone with Him.

A true self-knowledge

In his desperation Jacob had the heavenly visitor in a wrestling clinch that lasted all night. It is evidence of a profound intuition in Jacob that his moment of truth had dawned. Although the Angel had already dislocated his hip, Jacob's desperation gave rise to a continued strength which refused to release that One from the powerful wrestling clinch he had on Him. Jacob knew it was "now or never." "Let me go, for the day is breaking," the Angel cried, but Jacob said, "I will not let you go unless you bless me."

Why did the Man ask, "What is your name?" He not only knew the name of Jacob but had carefully arranged this meeting! Why then did the Lord ask this question? It seems to me that He wanted to settle a matter with Jacob once and for all. Had Jacob come to a genuine realization of what he was? Did he realize for the first time that the problem was in himself? Or would he "beat around the bush," making excuses for himself? In fact, Jacob had finally seen himself, and the knowledge of who he was and what he was, had devastated him. For the first time he saw *himself* as the problem. If it were not that the Lord was there, he would have been in total self-despair. Only God could change Jacob into Israel. No one else had either the power or the ability. In my estimation, it takes far more power to save and change a human being into the likeness of the Lord Jesus than to create the universe, or bring light out of darkness. God had brought Jacob to Jabbok, and Jacob was alone with the only One who had the determination, the grace, and the power to change him.

When the Lord asked Jacob what his name was, Jacob could have answered and said, "Me, I am Abraham's grandson." Or he could have said, "Isaac's son." Instead he answered, "Jacob." Jacob was sick of himself and owned up with a recognition of his nature and his history. I wonder if, in that single moment, Jacob thought, "This is the end." Instead the Lord said, "You shall no more be called Jacob, the twister, the grasper, but you shall be called Israel." As we have mentioned before, Israel means "God perseveres or persists." Indeed, if God had not persevered, Jacob would never have become Israel. There is, however, yet another side to this. For the Lord said, "You have striven with God ... and have prevailed." It was not only God who persevered and persisted, but, by the grace of God in him, Jacob the twister had also persevered. Such is the fathomless and invincible love of God.

A genuine self-knowledge through the Lord

It is interesting to note that Jacob never came to a genuine self-knowledge by introspection, or by placing himself under a microscope and studying his faults and weaknesses. It was not through some religious affliction of the flesh, through a harsh treatment of the body, or through a kind of spiritual "brain-washing" that he came to such an understanding of himself. It was through the Lord and the Lord's dealings with him. It is important to note that God principally used relationships with other people to bring Jacob to a genuine and healthy self-knowledge. Such knowledge of ourselves is essential, for as always the truth of God frees us. When in the light of the Lord, we begin to see ourselves as we really are, to understand what motivates us, and to recognize the hidden "soul force" in us, we are ready for our "Jabbok."

So few Christians know themselves

There is so little genuine self-knowledge amongst Christian believers. It is rare to find Christians, even servants of the Lord, who know themselves. I remember years ago a man writing to me and complaining bitterly about another brother. Both of them were very important men in a well-known Christian organization, but could not bear one another. He ended his letter, having exhaustively and negatively described the other brother, by the words, "You know that I am one of the most humble men in the world." Everyone who knew this gifted brother, recognized that his problem was that he was not humble. Yet he thought that everyone else was the problem. I remember another example. I had reproached a younger brother for his "big-headedness" and he answered, "I am ten times less big-headed this year than I was last year." The truth was different, for he was even more "big-headed." Or yet another example: there was a sister in the area in which I lived, a member of the same assembly, and she would often say, "You can tell me anything because I know how to keep a confidence." We all knew that if we wanted the whole town to know something, all we had to do was to speak to this sister and tell her that it was in confidence. Within hours everyone would know it! One could furnish a whole book with further examples!

Seeing ourselves in others

When the Lord brought Jacob to an honest and realistic understanding of himself, He used those nearest and dearest to him. He used Jacob's beloved mother, Rebecca. Jacob may have regretted his mother's deceitful strategy concerning his aged and nearly blind father, recognizing that his enforced exile from his home was caused by the deceit that was in her. I doubt whether he believed for a moment that it was in him as well. Many times Jacob must have thought of his mother and the event that forced him to leave her. He was not to see her again on this earth.

Jacob sees himself in Laban and Leah

The Lord also used Jacob's uncle, Laban. For twenty years the two of them double-crossed one another, and Jacob felt that he was the victim. At the beginning of Jacob's time with Laban, Laban appeared very generous. He gave no intimation that he would exploit Jacob. "You are my bone and my flesh," he declared. "What should your wages be?" Jacob had fallen in love with Rachel. In fact, she was *the* love of his life, and he never fell out of love with her. "I will work seven years for you, if you will give me Rachel as my wife." There are few husbands who would work seven years to obtain a wife, and that without a salary, unless there was a consuming and genuine love. It is touching that the record says that those seven years seemed to Jacob "but a few days, for the love he had to her." Laban apparently felt that Jacob was worth having as a son-in-law, and agreed.

One has to remember that in Oriental custom, especially in the Middle East, one cannot marry off a younger daughter before one has married off the elder; otherwise everyone will come to the conclusion that there is something wrong with the elder daughter, and she will be "left on the shelf." Laban's wife is not even mentioned in the record, but I can imagine her saying to him, "It's all very well for you to agree to this arrangement with Jacob, but what about poor Leah?" Laban probably thought that within those seven years someone would want to marry Leah and the problem would be solved. However, no one appeared. It must have been then that the deceitful scheme occurred to him to marry Leah to Jacob in place of Rachel.

Of course, it was not only Laban who worked this deceit, for Leah played an essential role in it. Laban and his wife must have said to her, "You must keep your mouth shut and imitate your sister in every way." The fact that she would have been veiled, that it was night, and the lights would have been dim, and that much wine would have been imbibed, would have all helped in the deception. Only the next morning did Jacob discover that it was Leah and not his beloved Rachel.

There is nothing more than an experience such as this to bring home to Jacob the nature of deception. He must have thought to himself, "How could my own uncle, my own flesh and blood, do such a thing to me? I have slaved for seven years to win Rachel, and I have been swindled!" Did the memory of the way he deceived his twin brother, Esau, come home to him at that point? Or did the memory of the deception of his old father, when he cheated Esau out of the blessing, then dawn on him? I think not! At that point he was unaware of himself. All he could think about was the way he had been cheated. It is interesting to observe that the Lord used those matters which are the most intimate and nearest to the heart, to confront Jacob with the deceit in his own heart. The fact that Jacob did not recognize himself at that point also reveals how incredibly tough and resilient a person can be.

One would have thought that the events of that night would have dampened Laban's business acumen. Laban showed no shame over his deception when Jacob confronted him the next day. "What is this you have done to me? Was it not for Rachel that I served with you? Why then have you deceived me?" Laban was not in the least ashamed and instead suggested that Jacob work another seven years for him. If he agreed, then when the normal seven days of Leah's wedding celebration were completed, Jacob could have Rachel as well. In other words there would be a further wedding celebration. There is no doubt that Jacob recognized his uncle's deceitful nature, his inability to restrain himself when he saw the possibility of a good deal. Twice Jacob spoke of the fact that Laban had cheated him and changed his wages ten times. It seems that Jacob had begun to recognize the ugly and destructive effect that an uncrucified self-life has on everyone. Whether at that point he recognized it within himself is another matter!

Jacob sees himself in Rachel

Rachel was the one person in Jacob's circle that he felt had no deceit. It is often said that love is blind. When, however, Jacob and his family left Paddan-Aram, Rachel stole her father's family gods. These household idols were the title deeds to property. Laban and the rest of the family were shearing the sheep when Rachel saw her opportunity to steal them. Apparently she felt that her father had cheated Leah and herself, and their children, as well as Jacob, out of what was rightfully theirs.

Laban was outraged when he found that they had all left for good, without so much as a word. To his outrage was added fury when he discovered that the household idols had been stolen. He gathered together a posse of men and overtook Jacob's entourage, and confronted Jacob. He reproached Jacob for leaving without so much as a word, and raised the matter of the household idols. Jacob was greatly angered that Laban should have thought that he placed any value on Laban's gods. He had no idea that Rachel had stolen them. "Search everything," he said, "and see if you can find them. With whomever you find the idols, that one shall not live." It is interesting to note that Laban did search everything. In the scriptural record it is recorded that Laban "felt" or "touched" everything in the tent. Rachel had said to him, "Do not ask me to get up for I am not feeling very well," and Laban left her. She was sitting on the camel saddle, and under the saddle were the household idols. It is a sad fact that Rachel died within months of this event.

As I have written already, Jacob saw himself first in Rebecca, then in Laban, then in Leah, and finally in his beloved Rachel. It was as if all of them became a mirror in which he saw himself. Sick of himself, he left Paddan-Aram and came to the river Jabbok. Behind him was Laban, and in front of him was Esau. It was the last stage in the Lord's preparation of Jacob. His fear of Esau, his self-despair, and the understanding of his real nature meant that he was ready finally for the Lord drastically to change him.

How does the Lord bring those he redeems to a genuine and healthy knowledge of themselves? How does He prepare us for our "Jabbok"? In the same way that He prepared Jacob. He makes the people with whom we live, the people with whom we work, those to whom we are related, the means of our preparation. They become the mirror in which, in the end, we see ourselves, and reach a genuine and realistic knowledge of ourselves. In the early stages of the Lord's dealings with us, we are often only aware of that which is wrong in others. Indeed, we become very critical of them and are unaware that in them we are seeing ourselves mirrored. Many children of God have fled from one uncomfortable and difficult situation, only to discover that they have ended in a worse one. It is the Lord! It is He who arranges the circumstances, the situations, and above all the relationships, and uses them to bring us to a true knowledge of ourselves.

The desperation of faith

> And Jacob was left alone; and there wrestled a man with him until the breaking of the day. And when he saw that he prevailed not against him, he touched the hollow of his thigh; and the hollow of Jacob's thigh was strained, as he wrestled with him. And he said, Let me go, for the day breaketh. And he said, I will not let thee go, except thou bless me. And he said unto him, What is thy name? And he said, Jacob. And he said, Thy name shall be called no more Jacob, but Israel: for thou hast striven with God and with men, and hast prevailed.
>
> (Gen. 32:24–28)

There is one other essential constituent. It is not enough to have a genuine and realistic knowledge of ourselves, or to be in self-despair. All of that is negative, even if it is indispensable. That further crucial constituent is living faith. I would describe it as the desperation of faith! A child of God who has never been in that place will be at a loss to understand what I am describing. On the other hand, those who have been there will understand. Self-despair produced by a true "seeing" of our self-life is not enough to change us from Jacob to Israel. It is the Lord alone who changes a Jacob into an Israel, not self-despair.

Only faith born of the Spirit of God within our dire condition joins us to the infinite power of the Almighty. It was the desperation of faith that caused Jacob to lay hold on the Lord in a wrestling clinch and cry, "I will not let you go except you bless me!" The Lord had already devastated him. Jacob's hip was dislocated and he would limp for the rest of his life, but he was Israel.

Margaret Barber's "Jabbok"

Margaret Barber, the missionary in China who had such a deep and lasting influence upon Watchman Nee's life and ministry, wrote a poem that vividly expresses this principle of brokenness, or lameness. Margaret Barber had an extraordinary influence upon the young women in the school in which she taught. Jealousy of her arose in the principal of the school and in some of the senior teachers. They accused her of serious character faults and unbecoming moral behavior. The rumors started by these few missionaries spread and, brokenhearted, she was forced to leave both the mission and her beloved China. She had lost her reputation, her fellowship with other believers, and even her practical relationship to China, to which she believed firmly that she had been called. She was "in pieces."

In Britain she went to see a godly bishop. He asked her, "Is there any truth in these accusations?" She replied, "None whatsoever." He then said, "Do you believe that the Lord has called you to China?" "I do," she replied. "Then," he said, "you shall go back to China with God, mission or no mission."

Margaret Barber returned with only God. She went back to the walled city in which she had lived, but decided to live outside of the walls, in a little place called "White Teeth Rock," where the great seafaring Tea Clippers used to dock. She began a Bible study to which a number of young men came. Within that group were those who would become well-known servants of the Lord, not only in China, but throughout the world. One

of them, and the most famous, was Watchman Nee. Margaret
Barber had probably no idea that out of her experience of
brokenness and devastation she would influence a whole nation.

In a violent storm, she watched helplessly as a ship was
wrecked. In her heart the Lord spoke: "This is what has
happened to you, but do not fear, for the wreck is in My
hand." Deeply moved, she wrote the words of this poem:

> "Wrecked outright on Jesus' breast:"
> Only "wrecked" souls thus can sing;
> Little boats that hug the shore,
> Fearing what the storm may bring,
> Never find on Jesus' breast,
> All that "wrecked" souls mean by rest.
>
> "Wrecked outright!" So we lament;
> But when storms have done their worst,
> Then the soul, surviving all,
> In Eternal arms is nursed;
> There to find that nought can move,
> One, embosomed in such love.
>
> "Wrecked outright!" No more to own
> E'en a craft to sail the sea;
> Still a voyager, yet now
> Anchored to Infinity;
> Nothing left to do but fling
> Care aside, and simply cling.
>
> "Wrecked outright!" 'Twas purest gain,
> Henceforth other craft can see,
> That the storm may be a boon,
> That, however rough the sea,
> God Himself doth watchful stand,
> For the "wreck" is in His hand.

This was Margaret Barber's Jabbok, and it "anchored her to infinity." She was the wreck in the hand of God, lost in His greatness and fullness. Everyone who knew her witnessed to the fact that they touched the Lord Himself when they touched her!

The apostle Peter's Jabbok

In the life of the chief apostle, Peter, we have another illustration of this. Some hours before he fell and denied the Lord three times with oaths, the Lord Jesus had said to him,

> Simon, Simon, behold, Satan asked to have you, that he might sift you as wheat: but I made supplication for thee, that thy faith fail not . . .
>
> (Luke 22:31–32; cf. Matt. 26:69–75)

We would probably describe Peter's experience at this point in his life as "the collapse of Peter's faith." In spite of the fact that Peter had walked with the Lord for more than three years and was recognized as the leader of the twelve apostles, his Christianity was self-manufactured. It was a mixture of genuine revelation and understanding, and a very powerful self-life. As with many of us, it was a mixture of the flesh and the Spirit. The Lord Jesus referred to this when He said, "Satan has obtained you by request that he might sift you as wheat." In other words there was in Peter a mixture of chaff and wheat, and Satan knew that fact. When Peter fell, his self-manufactured "Christian life and service" was blown away.

It was a spiritual nuclear explosion that cleared the ground of everything Peter had built on it. It was his Jabbok! He was devastated, dislocated, and in self-despair. Where, one could ask, was the faith that the Lord Jesus had spoken about? Yet it was there, buried under a religious façade. The Lord had said,

"I made supplication for thee, that *thy faith* fail not." It took only one look from the Lord when He turned His face toward Peter and their eyes met. Simon wept his way back to become Peter, or Cephas, a rock. Peter could have called this experience "Peniel," the face of God. It would have exactly described it. Satan had wanted to destroy Peter, but all he obtained was the chaff. God had obtained the wheat.

Charles Wesley's "Jabbok"

Charles Wesley wrote a magnificent hymn based on his own vivid experience. It is hardly ever sung today, even in its most shortened form. He had come to the same place that Jacob had come at Jabbok. He had gone to his room, shut the door, and said, "I will remain here until the Lord touches me." He wrote the hymn at intervals through the night, and when God did touch him and break him, he completed it. It embodies an experience all too rare today, but a necessary and essential experience if we are to reach the Lord's goal. Some of the language may seem dated, but it is best to keep it exactly as written:

Come, O thou Traveller unknown,
Whom still I hold, but cannot see!
My company before is gone,
And I am left alone with Thee;
With Thee all night I mean to stay,
And wrestle till the break of day.

I need not tell Thee who I am,
My misery and sin declare;
Thyself hast called me by my name,
Look on Thy hands, and read it there;
But who, I ask Thee, who art Thou?
Tell me Thy name, and tell me now.

In vain Thou strugglest to get free,
I never will unloose my hold!
Art Thou the Man that died for me?
The secret of Thy love unfold;
Wrestling, I will not let Thee go,
Till I Thy name, Thy nature know.

Yield to me now, for I am weak,
But confident in self-despair;
Speak to my heart, in blessings speak,
Be conquered by my instant prayer;
Speak, or Thou never hence shalt move,
And tell me if Thy Name is Love.

'Tis Love! 'tis Love! Thou diedst for me!
I hear Thy whisper in my heart;
The morning breaks, the shadows flee,
Pure, universal love Thou art;
To me, to all Thy mercies move;
Thy nature and Thy Name is Love.

Lame as I am, I take the prey,
Hell, earth, and sin, with ease o'ercome;
I leap for joy, pursue my way,
And as a bounding hart fly home,
Through all eternity to prove
Thy nature and Thy Name is Love.

Chapter 10

THE PRINCIPLE OF LAMENESS

Wherever we turn in the Word of God, we discover the same principle that is exemplified in the experience of Jacob at Jabbok. When in the desperation of faith, he had laid hold on the heavenly visitor, that One had disabled him. There can be no doubt that it was the Lord who gave Jacob the power to take hold of Him. It is therefore the more arresting that in Jacob's "prevailing over God," God broke the strength of his natural life.

In the Word of God a man's physical strength is considered to be centered in his thighs. When the Lord broke Jacob's natural strength, it was therefore his thigh that He touched, and it would have been his sciatic nerve that produced the pain. It was not a passing experience though painful, a mere temporary lack of ability. For the rest of Jacob's life he limped. In the story as recorded, it is spoken of as the "hollow of his thigh." That phrase could be translated as the "joint" or "socket" of his thigh. In fact, the Lord had dislocated his hip. It has to be of very great significance that the Lord, who would normally heal, in this instance crippled one of His servants.

What the Lord did to Jacob was so significant that when, by the Spirit of God, the writer of the letter to the Hebrews sums up Jacob's life, he writes, "By faith, Jacob ... worshipped, leaning upon the top of his staff" (11:21). The permanent

142

nature of Jacob's disability is revealed by his having to lean on his staff. Jacob the bargainer had become Jacob the worshiper; and Jacob the acquirer had become Jacob the one who could bless. It was the disabling of his natural power, the breaking of his self-life, which produced the ability to worship God, and to bless others. This principle lies at the heart of all of God's dealings with those He saves and redeems. David declares,

> The sacrifices of God are a broken spirit:
> A broken and a contrite heart, O God, Thou wilt not
>   despise.
>
> (Ps. 51:17)

Our understanding of this matter is made even more clear by Isaiah when he prophesied,

> For thus saith the high and lofty One that inhabiteth eternity, whose name is Holy: I dwell in the high and holy place, with him also that is of a contrite and humble spirit, to revive the spirit of the humble, and to revive the heart of the contrite.
>
> (Isa. 57:15)

And again:

> to this man will I look, even to him that is of a poor and of a contrite spirit, and that trembleth at my word.
>
> (Isa. 66:2)

The Hebrew word translated by the English word "contrite" comes from a root meaning "to break, to crush, to humble, to be broken in pieces, etc." The fact that the Almighty God speaks of dwelling, or making His home, in those who are crushed, who are broken, should never therefore be underestimated. He shuns the proud and the arrogant but makes His home with those who are weak.

When the apostle Paul sums up his whole exposition of the gospel in the Roman letter, he beseeches us to present our bodies as a living sacrifice, holy, acceptable to God, which is, he writes, our spiritually intelligent worship and service (Rom. 12:1). A living sacrifice surely betokens lameness or disability!

It is the same apostle who in another letter writes,

> always bearing about in the body the dying of Jesus, that the life also of Jesus may be manifested in our body. For we who live are always delivered unto death for Jesus' sake, that the life also of Jesus may be manifested in our mortal flesh. So then death worketh in us, but life in you.
>
> (2 Cor. 4:10–12)

This is what I mean by the term the principle of lameness!

Normally and rightly, Christians think of the saving and redeeming work of God as making us whole or sound. It is a healing and reconciling work that He performs. Clearly that is fundamental. Nevertheless, no believer will ever enjoy the full practical consequences of his or her salvation unless the self-life is first dealt with. In its unbroken state, it will *always* frustrate God's purpose for that life. For that reason alone, the Lord has always been in the business of "disabling" those whom He calls and saves. The end of the Lord, it should be emphasized, is not death or brokenness or being disabled: it is fullness of life, fullness of power, and fullness of fruit.

Consider some of the examples in the rest of the Bible:

Abraham

Abraham is rightly called "the father of all who believe." There is no question about his salvation through faith, or of his being made whole. Yet this one, of whom the Lord had said his seed would be in number "as the stars of the heavens ... and as the sand of the seashore" (see Gen. 22:17), was childless until nearly a hundred years of age. His calling was two-fold: to possess a land and to produce a seed, a numerous family. According to ancient Jewish tradition, Abraham came from the ruling class of Ur of the Chaldees; he was an aristocrat, whose father headed an idol-making business and owned much property. Abraham apparently acted as a salesman in the family business! When he left Ur, he left everything behind him to become a nomad, shepherding sheep, goats, and camels. He never owned a single yard or meter of the land promised to him as an eternal inheritance, except for one burial plot in Hebron. The self-contained and self-sufficient Abraham, with the kind of self-confidence we associate with salesmen, in obedience to God went out in faith not even knowing where he was going. He became not a land-owner but a pilgrim and a sojourner! From that point onwards he was utterly dependent upon the Lord. I would describe that as the principle of lameness in action.

This principle of disability is even more clearly seen in the fact that Abraham was childless. He was eighty-six years of age when Ishmael was born, not of promise but of worldly wisdom. God in fact made a covenant with Hagar and Ishmael, which over the ages He has kept to the letter. Nevertheless, the whole purpose of God was centered not in Ishmael, but in Isaac (Gen. 17:15–21; cf. 22:2). Abraham was ninety-nine years of age when Isaac was born. Those two sons can hardly be described as being like the stars of the heaven for multitude! Abraham's aristocratic relatives must have thought of him as "poor old Abram, childless and landless." After all, two children in the Middle East are hardly considered a family. He had left much property, and a large and lucrative business, to wander as a nomad. His walk with the Lord then, of necessity, had to be a walk of faith. The Lord disabled Abraham's self-confidence, his trust in his own power and energy. He broke Abraham's reliance on his own wisdom and capability. He had made Abraham dependent upon Himself.

Joseph

In the life of Joseph again we see this principle in action. The Lord had given Joseph dreams (see Gen. 37:5–11). There is no doubt that it was the Lord, even if the manner in which Joseph had recounted them was precocious and arrogant. Those dreams were all related to the divine calling of Joseph. He was indeed destined to be the savior of Egypt as also of his family. Jacob described Joseph as "a fruitful bough, A fruitful bough by a fountain: His branches run over the wall" (Gen. 49:22). It was an apt summary of Joseph's life and calling: Joseph was not only the savior of his family but also of Egypt.

Nevertheless, the way to that fulfillment was to be through slavery and prison. In those difficult years of affliction, it is said,

> His soul entered into the iron, until the time that his word came to pass, the word of the LORD tried him.
>
> (Ps. 105:18–19 mg)

I would describe this as the disabling of the unusually gifted and capable Joseph. There can be no question about Joseph's calling or about his gifts, but the way to the fulfillment of God's purpose for him was brokenness. It is again the principle of lameness in action.

Moses

Once more we see this same principle in Moses. Brought up as Pharaoh's grandson within the royal palace, with the quality and standards of education and training afforded by such a position, God had preserved him with an especial calling in mind. The New Testament describes Moses as being "instructed in all the wisdom of the Egyptians ... mighty in his words and works" (Acts 7:22). It also speaks of him "accounting the reproach of the Messiah greater riches than the treasures of Egypt" (Heb. 11:26).

These two sparse New Testament references nonetheless give a picture of his status, his ability, and his talent. According to Jewish tradition Moses was highly decorated for his military prowess in the Ethiopian military campaign, and as a result was a popular folk hero. The name Moses in Hebrew is once again a play on words. Literally it means "a draw-er out." It seems, however, that Pharaoh's daughter called him "Moses" because *she* drew him out of the water (see Exod. 2:10). As so often in the Bible it was prophetic of his calling. It was not only that he himself was preserved, "drawn out" of the water; he was also to be the God-given deliverer of the children of Israel from Egypt. He would be the leader whom the Lord would use to "draw out" His redeemed people.

For the fulfillment of that call, the strong, capable, and gifted Moses nevertheless had to be disabled! The Lord used goats and sheep and forty years in the backside of the desert to disable him. It is a fact that the herding of goats and sheep was a horror to the Egyptian aristocracy.

When the Lord met Moses in a dried-up and dead thorn-bush, it was a picture of Moses and the Lord. The fire was the symbol of the Lord, and the dead thorn-bush the symbol of Moses. When the fire and the bush came together, the purpose of God would be fulfilled. "The bush burned with fire, and the bush was not consumed" (Exod. 3:2). To reduce Moses from a stately and royal palm tree to a worthless, dried-up and dead thorn-bush is surely the principle of lameness in action.

It is a source of continual amazement to me that it was when the Lord was "in the bush," that He revealed His name as "I AM that I AM." It was as if the Lord said, "I AM the Infinite, the All-seeing, the All-knowing, the always Present God, the Uncreated, the All-sufficient One, and in you I AM everything you will ever need." The thorn-bush was not even alive but dead. Its natural resources had been exhausted. It was finished. Only the God of all grace would dwell in such a bush, through it revealing Himself, and by it fulfilling His purpose! Once Moses was reduced to such a condition, God could fulfill His purpose through him, and did so!

David

David is one of the principal characters in the Bible. It is impossible to read the Word of God without recognizing his importance and significance. He is at the heart of the fulfillment of God's purpose. From his lineage came the Messiah, "great David's greater son." Indeed, with the Lord Jesus, King of Israel, King of kings, the house of David will never disappear! As Isaiah prophesies,

> For unto us a child is born, unto us a son is given; and the government shall be upon his shoulder: and his name shall be called Wonderful, Counsellor, Mighty God, Everlasting Father, Prince of Peace. Of the increase of his government and of peace there shall be no end, upon the throne of David, and upon his kingdom, to establish it, and to uphold it with justice and with righteousness from henceforth even forever.
>
> (Isa. 9:6–7)

When Samuel the prophet was deeply disillusioned with King Saul, mourning over the lack of spiritual character in him, the Lord revealed to him the man who would be king in Saul's place. In Bethlehem, in the midst of David's family, long before he became king, Samuel anointed David as king.

David was the youngest of Jesse's eight sons, a simple, unknown shepherd boy, albeit gifted and capable (see 1 Sam. 16:1–13). It was a God-given victory over Goliath, the hero of the Philistines, which brought David to fame in Israel. He became a popular folk hero, a confidant of the king, and the closest friend of Jonathan, the king's son and crown prince.

David was an interesting combination of physical prowess, genuine musical and poetic ability, and spiritual understanding.

From an early age he had revealed an exceptional gift. He came to be called "the sweet psalmist of Israel." Whilst King Saul was bitterly jealous of David's popularity as the victor over the Philistines, he greatly valued his musical gift, and included David in the "royal circle." David apparently never revealed Samuel's secret anointing of himself to Saul.

Knowing the Middle East, however, I imagine that the news had circulated through Bethlehem and far beyond it. It would have been impossible in a large family such as David's, living close to others in a small community, for that event not to have been known, or for rumors not to begin. The fact that someone as famous as Samuel had suddenly appeared in Bethlehem, and visited one particular family, would have insured this.

What is certainly true is that King Saul saw in David a threat and became ever more deeply possessed of a demonic and violent jealousy. On a number of occasions he sought to murder David, and David became a hunted refugee for twenty years. In all of those years he was without standing or rank, homeless, and pursued from place to place. In order to survive he had to live in caves, or inaccessible crags, or remote places in the wilderness. Far from being a king, he was the leader of a bunch of men that were in debt, in distress, or discontented (see 1 Sam. 22:2). Where was the fulfillment of his divine calling? I would describe this as the principle of disability, of lameness.

Out of this experience of loneliness, of harassment, of misrepresentation, and of maltreatment, David finally emerged as king. Many of his most-loved psalms came out of this experience of "nothingness." They are the evidence of spiritual character produced by the Spirit of God in deep affliction and brokenness, and in incredibly difficult conditions.

Gideon

When the Lord reduced the great number that had rallied to Gideon, first from 32,000 to 10,000, and then from 10,000 to 300, you have this same principle once again demonstrated. The Midianites, the Amalekites, and the children of the East were, we are told, of enormous number. Humanly speaking, Gideon needed every one of those 32,000 men. With so few men, there was no way that he could defeat such numerous enemies. The Lord's strategy was quite different. He had said that He wanted to reduce them "lest Israel vaunt themselves against me, saying, Mine own hand hath saved me."

It is significant that the plan given by the Lord to Gideon was to divide the 300 men into three groups, to give them empty pitchers, torches, and trumpets. When Gideon blew his trumpet, they were all to blow their trumpets, to break the pitchers and hold up the torches. The torches would not have had enough oxygen in the enclosed pitchers; only when the pitchers were broken would the torches fully ignite. It is another illustration of this principle of brokenness.

Through this amazing strategy, God gave a resounding victory (see Judg. 7:1–22). To reduce an army from 32,000 to 300, and to arm them with nothing more than a pitcher, a torch, and a trumpet, is by this world's standards nonsensical. With such a strategy, no one on this earth would ever expect a great victory! Yet a trumpet, a broken pitcher, and the light of fire were the only requirements the Lord demanded for victory. The Lord has the same requirements today: the uncompromised and confessed Word of the Lord, utter brokenness, and the fire of the Holy Spirit. It is a vivid illustration of the words of Isaiah, "the lame take the prey" (see Isa. 33:23 KJV).

Barrenness

It is noteworthy that it required a miracle for many of the greatest characters in the Bible to be born. Their mothers had a problem with barrenness. Consider Sarah and the birth of Isaac; or Rebecca and the birth of Esau and Jacob; or Rachel and the birth of Joseph and Benjamin; or Hannah and the birth of

Samuel; or Elizabeth and the birth of John the Baptist. Barrenness is a form of lameness and disability. Whenever the Lord acts to fulfill a purpose of His, He makes the circumstances difficult; but whenever He plans something exceptional, He makes the situation impossible. Then when His purpose is fulfilled, in spite of the impossibility, all the glory goes to Him.

In all these characters, which I have selected from many more that could have been mentioned, there was an unbroken natural self-life. It expressed itself in different ways. Abraham was very different from Jacob, as was Joseph, or Moses, or David, or Gideon, or the mothers of Israel. Yet in the life of every one of them, we see the same basic principle in action. The Lord worked to disable their natural life and ability, so that He could fulfill His purpose through them.

Rivers of living water

On the last day of the feast of Tabernacles, *Sukkot*, "the great day," the Levites poured out water on the steps leading from the women's court to the court of Israel. It was an immensely popular ritual, a ceremony that illustrated the unfulfilled promise of the pouring out of the Holy Spirit on all flesh. It was on that day Jesus stood and declared,

> If any man thirst, let him come unto me and drink. He that believeth on me, as the scripture hath said, from within him shall flow rivers of living water.
>
> (John 7:37–38)

It is one thing to come and drink of the water of life that He gives; it is another matter when there is a spiritual watershed within the believer. On the one hand, the thirst of the believer is quenched either initially or many times subsequently. On the other hand, the believer becomes a spring of resurrection life and power. The source of the rivers of living waters is within him or her!

The Lord Jesus did not say *a river* of living water would flow out of the one who believes in Him, but *rivers* of living water. Anyone who has seen the power of a little water to turn a desert place into fertility and fruitfulness, has to be challenged by this declaration. Yet the Lord was not speaking here of a stream, or a rivulet, but of mighty rivers! There is no end to the possibilities and potentialities of a life that becomes a spiritual watershed, in which the Holy Spirit is free to glorify the Lord Jesus. In such a believer the Holy Spirit, ungrieved, unquenched, and unfettered, is released. Such mighty rivers, however, can only flow out if the vessel is broken!

The problem for most of us is simple. Those rivers of living water are dammed up in an unbroken vessel. All the life-giving power is blocked at its source, and the effective barrier is an unbroken self-life. The result is always the same; instead of abundant fruitfulness, the life of that Christian is an unfruitful, infertile desert. It is barrenness. A self-life can be pleasant, decent, apparently modest, and even devoutly religious, masking nonetheless a self-seeking and self-centered life. On the other hand, a self-life can be assertive, aggressive, and ugly; and everyone recognizes it for its true nature. In whatever manner it manifests itself, it will always successfully dam up the rivers of living water, unless it is broken. That self-life has to be laid down. There is no alternative! Samuel Rutherford, the Scottish Divine, when in prison for his faith said, "Men want Christ cheap. They want Him without the cross, but the price will not come down."

The apostle Paul

The apostle Paul is another example but this time in the New Testament. He lived and served on this principle. He wrote that the Lord had said to him,

My grace is sufficient for thee: for my power is made perfect in weakness.

And he continued,

Most gladly therefore will I rather glory in my weaknesses, that the power of Christ may rest upon me. Wherefore I take pleasure in weaknesses, in injuries, in necessities, in persecutions, in distresses, for Christ's sake: for when I am weak, then am I strong.

(2 Cor. 12:9–10)

He recognized that God used all the circumstances and problems of his life to bring him to the place of "weakness," so that the glorious and infinite power of the Messiah might tabernacle upon him. Consider the list he records: weaknesses, injuries, necessities, persecutions, and distresses. Many Christians would hardly consider that to be a description of the normal Christian life! Indeed, they would consider Paul in need of counseling! Yet in this testimony we have a window into the heart of the apostle.

Paul's experience is a further illustration of the principle of disability or lameness. Whatever the thorn in the flesh was, it was a messenger of Satan, a satanic angel. Paul never revealed what the problem was, but he recognized it as a most serious threat to his ministry and to his spiritual life and ability. When this letter was written, he had already besought the Lord three times to remove the problem. The only answer the Lord gave to Paul was that His grace was sufficient for him, and that divine power can only be brought to fullness in weakness. This was Paul's Jabbok! It was the face and the presence of God. He came to understand that in his weakness the power of the Messiah tabernacled upon him. The simple but profound testimony he gave was that when he was weak in himself, then he was strong in the Lord. Sadly, many of us are too strong in ourselves for the Lord to use us.

In this matter, the apostle Paul had an ongoing experience of the grace of God, out of which so many of his letters were written. Any servant of the Lord who has been "disabled" has the same experience of the grace of God. This is the principle of lameness in action. In all probability, much of Paul's understanding of this principle came through the "thorn in the flesh" given to him by the Lord.

The Son of Man

We cannot speak of the Messiah, our Lord Jesus, in the same manner as we have spoken of these other characters. He never needed to be changed. There was no Jacob in Him that needed to be transformed into Israel. He was the New Man, the Last Adam, and the Second Man (see 1 Cor. 15:45, 47; Col. 3:10–11). Nevertheless, we see this principle of lameness clearly demonstrated in Him. The writer of the Hebrew letter, for example, declares,

> For it became him, for whom are all things, and through whom are all things, in bringing many sons unto glory, to make the author of their salvation perfect through sufferings.
>
> (2:10)

And again he writes,

> though he was a Son, yet learned obedience by the things which he suffered; and having been made perfect, he became unto all them that obey him the author of eternal salvation.
>
> (5:8–9)

The Greek word here translated "perfect" can be also translated "complete" or "mature." Even the Lord Jesus, who was without sin, as a man was brought to complete maturity, or to full development, through "the things which he suffered."

It is amazing to recognize that it was God Himself who was born of a woman. The apostle John wrote,

> In the beginning was the Word, and the Word was with God, and the Word was God. The same was in the beginning with God. All things were made through him; and without him was not anything made that hath been made. In him was life ... And the Word became flesh, and dwelt among us...
>
> (John 1:1–4, 14)

This is the mystery of the incarnation! If it were not so clearly stated in God's Word, it would be difficult to accept. At Bethlehem He was born a babe, a mere foot of human flesh and blood, cradled in the arms of a young woman, a teenager and a virgin.

It is well nigh impossible for us to understand that the Living God, the Infinite, the Uncreated, reduced Himself to such weakness and became dependent upon a human being for sustenance and protection. In those early months, He could not even move around without human help. In every way, the infinite power of God was centered in that weakness. Could one reverently describe it as the principle of disability? It is surely a demonstration of the words of the apostle Paul, "the weakness of God is stronger than men" (1 Cor. 1:25).

Writing about the Lord Jesus, Paul declared:

> [He], existing in the form of God, counted not the being on an equality with God a thing to be grasped, but emptied himself, taking the form of a servant, being made in the likeness of men; and being found in fashion as a man, he humbled himself, becoming obedient even unto death, yea, the death of the cross.
>
> (Phil. 2:6–8)

The word here translated "servant" is not the "house-servant" but the "bond-slave." It is almost incomprehensible that the

Lord, who was on an equality with God, became a bond-slave in order to win our salvation! In the ancient world, the bond-slave was the lowest stratum of human society; he or she basically had no rights. Surely this again illustrates the principle of "lameness." Here we are face to face with divine mystery, forever beyond our finite minds. However, this we know, that He, by becoming a bond-slave, saved us through the work He accomplished on the cross.

Indeed, it is at Calvary that we see most clearly this principle. Paul states that the Lord Jesus "was crucified through weakness" (2 Cor. 13:4). When the Lord Jesus was most disabled – flogged, famished, dehydrated, and nailed to a tree – the power of God to win our salvation was most manifest. That was the point at which darkness came over the earth.

It was not an eclipse, for no eclipse can last for three hours. Something happened to the basic energy of the universe, as if a sword had pierced through it, as if for a moment it was paralyzed. In my estimation, that essential energy is the life of God Himself. It is here that we stand in the presence of fathomless mystery. None of us will ever fully understand what happened when the Lamb of God bore away the sins of the world: when He became the uplifted serpent (John 1:29; cf. 3:14–15). What we know with certainty is that the Lord Jesus took the poison of the serpent and bore it away into oblivion, that He might save us and deliver us.

We should never dwell on the physical side of the cross. That is to miss the profound significance of what the Messiah accomplished there. It is noteworthy that the eyewitness accounts of the crucifixion in the gospels never magnify the physical aspects of it. The real pain, the genuine suffering, was in His becoming sin for us. That was in another dimension, in the invisible, far beyond our human understanding! We only see the physical evidences – the nails, the dehydration, the dislocation of His bones, etc. When, however, Jesus bore away the sin of the world, when He who knew no sin, became sin for us, the whole universe shuddered. It was in that moment that He cried out in utter weakness, "My God, my God, why hast Thou forsaken me?"

When He came to the point of His most extreme brokenness, power greater than any nuclear power this world knows, was released. *He had won!* In those six hours, the Lord Jesus, in utter weakness, won for sinful man an eternal salvation. The crucified Messiah, the disabled Messiah, the One crucified in weakness, became the power of God to save any man or woman who puts their trust in Him, however hopeless, depraved, or sinful their condition.

At the exact moment that He cried out in triumph, "finished," the great veil in the temple, dividing the Holy Place from the Most Holy, was torn in two from top to bottom. Sinful man and a holy God were reconciled! There has never been before, or since, such power displayed. The power to create the universe, to bring light out of darkness, to create life in its many forms, is kindergarten power compared to the power required to save sinful mankind.

At Calvary we see this principle of lameness, of brokenness, of weakness in action. It lies at the heart of our salvation. It is summed up in the matchless words of the apostle Paul: "we preach Christ crucified ... Christ the power of God, and the wisdom of God" (1 Cor. 1:23a, 24b).

Chapter 11

JACOB THE OVERCOMER

The Lame Takes the Prey

And God appeared unto Jacob again, when he came from
Paddan-aram, and blessed him. And God said unto him, Thy
name is Jacob: thy name shall not be called any more Jacob, but
Israel shall be thy name: and he called his name Israel. And God
said unto him, I am God Almighty: be fruitful and multiply; a
nation and a company of nations shall be of thee, and kings shall
come out of thy loins; and the land which I gave unto Abraham
and Isaac, to thee I will give it, and to thy seed after thee will I
give the land. And God went up from him in the place where he
spake with him ... And Jacob called the name of the place
where God spake with him, Bethel [the house of God].

(Gen. 35:9–13, 15)

When Jacob returned to Bethel from Paddan-Aram, he was a
different man. The Lord had done something in him that was to
affect the rest of his life. It is therefore of great interest to note
that at the point when he stepped back into the promised land,
the Lord met him with the same words He had spoken to him
at Jabbok:

Thy name is Jacob: thy name shall not be called any more
Jacob, but Israel shall be thy name.

The Lord then underlines all the matters about which I have
written: fruitfulness; multiplication; possessing the land; and
the house of God. It is spiritually significant that this happened
at Bethel, the place where he first had the revelation concerning
God's house.

There is a remarkable prophecy recorded in Isaiah:

> But there the LORD will be with us in majesty, a place of broad
> rivers and streams, wherein shall go no galley with oars,
> neither shall gallant ship pass thereby. For the LORD is our
> judge, the LORD is our lawgiver, the LORD is our king; he will
> save us. Thy tacklings are loosed; they could not strengthen
> the foot of their mast, they could not spread the sail: then
> was the prey of a great spoil divided; the lame took the prey.
>
> (Isa. 33:21–23)

There is a little phrase which expresses the rest of Jacob's life till
he went to be with the Lord, "the lame took the prey."

It is interesting that this phrase is found in a passage which
begins with, "Thine eyes shall see the king in his beauty"
(v. 17a). It was certainly true of Jacob. He had seen the King in
His beauty and was a changed man. He was indeed lame, and he
had begun to take the prey. On any account the phrase itself is
extraordinary. It seems an odd and strange thing to say! We do
not normally think of somebody who is crippled winning a race,
let alone fighting enemies and taking the prey. In fact, we would
normally consider a lame person incapable of winning anything.
With God it is totally different. Jacob with his dislocated hip,
limping for the rest of his earthly life, in the end wins the race
and gains the prize. The lame Jacob takes the prey! By disabling
him, the purpose of God in Jacob was secured.

The Lord did extraordinary things with this man. For such is
the depth and extent of the undying power and perseverance of
God's love. In order to reach the goal of His election, He
crippled him and made it impossible for him to be the same

again. The hand of God had disabled Jacob's spontaneous natural strength, the tremendous power of his soul's personality, and the fund of natural energy that was in him. He was indeed "a vessel afore prepared by God unto glory." It cost the Lord everything, even His death on the cross, to conform Jacob to His likeness. It also cost Jacob everything!

Jacob when he was dying, blessed . . . and worshiped

The last picture we have of Jacob is of an old saint bowing his head and worshiping God as he died. He was 147 years of age. He was lame and disabled to the very end, for we are told by the Holy Spirit that he was leaning on his staff:

> By faith Jacob, when he was dying, blessed each of the sons of Joseph; and worshipped, leaning upon the top of his staff.
>
> (Heb. 11:21)

This is the Greek of the LXX; the Hebrew says that he worshiped "upon the bed's head." Apparently he pulled himself up on the bedpost and worshiped the Lord just before he died. Whether leaning on his staff, or holding on to the bedpost, the last picture is the same. It indicates Jacob's lameness. The bargainer had become the worshiper of God in spirit and in truth; the acquirer had become the one who blesses others; the disabled Jacob had become, by the grace of God, an overcomer. Thus the New Testament sums up the end of God's dealings with Jacob as making him an overcomer, a blessing to others, and a true worshiper of the Lord.

Jacob, the one who blesses

God had done something so deep, so radical, and so complete that this man who stole blessings from others was able to bless everyone. He blessed his grandsons, he blessed his sons, he blessed Pharaoh, and thus Egypt. When this wonderful old man came to the end of his life, he was recognized as a blessing to Egypt. At his death we are told that the Egyptians turned out in their thousands to mourn him. Jacob was embalmed in the Egyptian manner and the normal forty days of official mourning was declared for the nation. Pharaoh sent a huge company of Egyptians, with all the official paraphernalia, to escort the coffin back to the promised land. The locals, at that time the Canaanite inhabitants of the land, were so impressed that they called the place where the Egyptians encamped *Abelmizraim*, "the field of Egypt" (see Gen. 50:1–14). Jacob's funeral was, for all intents and purposes, a state funeral. Who would have believed that Jacob, who stole everyone's blessings, became a blessing even to the unsaved. Some deep intuition within the pagan Egyptians recognized that Jacob stood at the heart of divine history.

The purpose of God for us as His children is that, like Jacob, we should become a blessing to everyone. The problem is that many of us steal the blessings. On the one hand, we are serving the Lord, contributing to the life of the church, and seeking to win others; and on the other hand, we are destroying everything we do and build. The problem is the same as Jacob's problem. It is an uncrucified, unbroken self-life handling the things of God. Only when the Lord deals with us, do we become the blessing He intends us to be.

Jacob, the worshiper of the Lord

Furthermore, until he came to Jabbok, Jacob was the antithesis of a worshiper. He was not by nature a worshiper. It did not belong to his "makeup," to his character, or to his personality. He was far too self-conscious and self-centered truly to worship God. It is highly significant that the very last picture we have of this man is of one who worships the Lord. God did such a deep work in Jacob that he became a worshiper in spirit and in truth:

no longer conscious of himself; only conscious of God and conscious of the need of others.

A self-centered person can never be a true worshiper. If you cannot open your mouth and really worship the Lord, or even worship the Lord in the quietness of your own heart, it is because you cannot forget yourself. No person can ever become a worshiper who is bound by such self-consciousness. If the heart of everything for you is yourself, if your whole understanding of the Christian life and service is only related to yourself, you can never worship. You cannot worship when you are full of your own aches and pains, your own problems, and your own needs. You could then *only* worship Him if and when He answers those needs.

You can take part in singing, be emotionally excited, and believe that you are worshiping. Singing, music, and emotion are all part of true worship, but they are after all the most shallow part. Real worship carries a person outside of themselves into a deep consciousness of God. If that element is missing, the rest of these things become superficial. God works such a deep work in true worshipers that they are lost in Him and forget themselves. Even though they know themselves, they are able to worship the Lord in love and adoration.

In its deepest form, worship is a life laid down for God. When the apostle Paul, in practical terms, begins to sum up his whole exposition of the gospel, he writes,

> I beseech you therefore, brethren, by the mercies of God, to present your bodies a living sacrifice, holy, acceptable to God, which is your spiritual service.
>
> (Rom. 12:1)

Paul's appeal is that our salvation should result practically in being "a living sacrifice." He was referring to the burnt offering, which symbolized that the life and service of the believer should be wholly given to God. It was a sacrifice totally burnt up! Such an appeal sounds strange to modern ears. As remarkable are the words "which is your spiritual service." The fact that this has been translated in slightly different ways in a number of the modern versions underlines the difficulty of the Greek. It is best understood as "which is your spiritually intelligent service and worship." It could also be translated as "tangible worship and service," i.e. worship and service expressed in its most tangible form. I have written that this is the deepest form of worship, and it is. Here we are at the heart of this matter. Nothing else will satisfy God.

After Jabbok, Jacob became a true worshiper. Jacob shines with the beauty of the Lord, and there is nothing now to obscure that testimony. Psalm 47:4 speaks of "the glory of Jacob." What is Jacob's glory? Surely it is the Lord Himself! It was the glory of the Lord that now shone through Jacob. In himself Jacob had been inglorious; there was so little that could be glorified. It was the persistent and persevering love of God that brought Jacob to glory, and it will also be true of us. True worship and the glory of God belong to each other. God's purpose for Jacob was always that he should become a worshiper. The fulfillment of that purpose took many years to accomplish. The Lord has the same purpose for us. Never forget the words of the Lord Jesus, that God seeks those who will be worshipers of the Father, in spirit and in truth (see John 4:23–24). The fulfillment of that purpose may take a lifetime to accomplish, but the Lord is faithful. He won the battle with Jacob; He will also win it with us!

Jacob the overcomer

By the Spirit of God, Jacob had become an overcomer. Overcoming is one of the great themes of the Bible. From God's simple command in the first chapter of Genesis to "have dominion...," we follow this theme throughout the Word of God until we come to Revelation 21:7, "he that overcometh shall inherit these things." In Hebrews chapters 11–12 we have a list of those who by faith became overcomers, from Abel to all of us who are saved by the grace of God in this present age. That list of overcomers both then and now is summed up by the words,

> but ye are come unto mount Zion, and unto the city of the living God, the heavenly Jerusalem, and to innumerable hosts of angels, to the general assembly and church of the firstborn who are enrolled in heaven, and to God the Judge of all, and to the spirits of just men made perfect, and to Jesus the mediator of a new covenant, and to the blood of sprinkling that speaketh better than that of Abel.
>
> (12:22–24)

We have a striking commentary on these chapters in the first letter of John:

> For whatsoever is begotten of God overcometh the world: and this is the victory that hath overcome the world, even our faith. And who is he that overcometh the world, but he that believeth that Jesus is the Son of God?
>
> (5:4–5)

The declaration made earlier in John's letter only underlines this truth:

> Ye are of God, my little children, and have overcome them: because greater is he that is in you than he that is in the world.
>
> (4:4)

What is overcoming?

What is overcoming? An overcomer is not an elitist, some superior being who knows that he is superior and looks down on other believers as second-class believers. Neither is an overcomer someone who by their nature, background, and personality is better than the poorer material found in the rest of us. An overcomer is one who in spite of all their failings and weaknesses is still found in the race, on course and within the will of God, at the end of their earthly life.

Many years ago when I was in the Scottish home of Theodore Austin-Sparks, this matter of overcoming came up in discussion. I asked him, "What is overcoming?" He looked at me for a moment and said, in a way only Mr Sparks could say, "Overcoming? Overcoming is that you are still in the race at the end." I have never forgotten that answer. There are many who begin the race but do not finish it; many who begin in the Spirit but end in the flesh. Overcoming is to discover in experience the grace and power of God made available to us. That grace and power is made a reality through the Person of the Holy Spirit, who keeps us on course, in spite of our faults, our weaknesses, and even our sins, once those sins have been confessed.

The book of Revelation, so complex to many believers, is the summing up of the sixty-six books of the Bible. It is, therefore, of real significance that it speaks of overcoming more than any other book. When the risen and glorified Messiah, in the midst of the seven churches, chosen to represent the whole true Church of God on earth, in time and in place, speaks to His own, He sums up His message by saying to each of the churches, "he that overcomes..." (Rev. 2:7, 11, 17, 26; 3:5, 12, 21).

Whatever view we hold concerning the twelfth chapter of Revelation, the practical message is the same. In the midst of this war in heaven, between the archangel Michael and his angels on the one hand and Satan on the other, we are told, "they overcame him by the blood of the Lamb, and because of the word of their testimony; and they loved not their lives even unto death" (v. 11). There is no other way to overcome than this. We have here three foundational aspects of overcoming: firstly, the blood of the Lamb, the finished and complete work of the Lord Jesus on the cross; secondly, the expression of the testimony of Jesus which we hold. This testimony is that "Jesus is Lord," and that in Him all the fullness of the Godhead dwells in bodily form; and we are complete in Him. It has to be confessed in an uncompromising manner. Thirdly, they loved not their lives even unto death: the losing of our self-life for His sake and the gospel's.

We have the same idea in the seventeenth chapter of Revelation. In the huge conflict between the Beast and the Lamb, in which we in the twenty-first century are involved, we have this marvelous statement:

> These shall war against the Lamb, and the Lamb shall over-come them, for he is Lord of lords, and King of kings; and they also shall overcome that are with him, called and chosen and faithful.
>
> (v. 14)

Carefully note that those who overcome "are with Him," and they are "called, chosen, and faithful." We are called and chosen but the practical challenge is whether we are faithful.

Called to be overcomers

From these references in the book of Revelation, we draw one vital lesson. By the grace of God and the gift of living faith, we are called to be overcomers. The truth is simple. We cannot be overcomers without *the* Overcomer. The Lord Jesus declared,

> These things have I spoken to you that in me ye may have peace. In the world ye have tribulation; but be of good cheer; I have overcome the world.
>
> (John 16:33)

The key to overcoming lies here. Christ is the Overcomer, and in us He is greater than Satan who is in the world (see 1 John 4:4). As the apostle Paul wrote,

> Nay, in all these things we are more than conquerers through him that loved us.
>
> (Rom. 8:37)

When Christ the Overcomer, by the Holy Spirit, dwells as Lord and life in a believer, the consequence is overcoming. It is a living principle; it is cause and effect.

Our overcoming is of tremendous importance to the Lord. The Word of God ends with a revelation of the heavenly Jerusalem. It is a remarkable union of two quite different ideas: a capital city; and a bride. Only the Holy Spirit could have brought these two ideas together and thus completed the revelation of God's eternal purpose in the Bible. From this picture we see the Lord is seeking two things in one: candidates for eternal government; and those that are in love with Him and enjoy deep union and communion with Him.

Reigning with Christ

There are not so many who come to the throne. There is an "if" in this matter. The Word of God says, "If we suffer, we shall also reign with him" (2 Tim. 2:12 KJV). Why is there this uncertainty? Why is there an "if"? It is because this matter of reigning is not merely a matter of being converted, of being forgiven, or of being justified. Those matters are foundational. The matter of reigning, however, is directly related to deep, inward spiritual history and experience. No one can come to the throne who does not have this character. For this reason the Lord speaks so much about "reigning." We have to learn to overcome and reign with the Messiah in our present, everyday experience on this earth. Sometimes we have mountainous obstacles and problems to face and overcome. On other occasions, it is the mundane, and the "humdrum" irritations and difficulties that defeat us. How we overcome in these matters is directly related to reigning with Christ in the ages to come.

Babies and little children cannot reign practically

Babes cannot reign practically. There has to be a certain minimal growth and maturity to reign! God's "problem" is that His family is filled with babes and little children who never grow up. He has a family, who for the most part are content to be an eternal kindergarten. His purpose for us, however, is that we should grow up to become good soldiers of His, to be sons who can administer the kingdom with Him, to be the fully mature bride and companion of the Lord Jesus, and thus be able to reign with Him.

Even our Lord Jesus "learned obedience by the things which he suffered," and thus was made perfect (Heb. 5:8–9). The Greek word translated "perfect" means "to be brought to full development or maturity." We have the same thought in Hebrews 2:10,

> For it became him, for whom are all things, and through whom are all things, in bringing many sons unto glory, to make the author of their salvation perfect through sufferings.

If the Lord of glory Himself, who "knew no sin," needed to learn obedience by the discipline of suffering and had to grow to maturity, to full development, through such sufferings, how much more do we who were born in sin?

The Lord Jesus declared,

> He that overcometh, I will give to him to sit down with me in my throne, as I also overcame, and sat down with my Father in his throne.

> (Rev. 3:21)

Carefully note the words "as I also overcame, and sat down
with my Father in his throne." The One who knew no sin, still
had to overcome and sit down in His Father's throne. In order
for us to sit down with Him in His throne, we also have to
overcome. The idea that we will sit on a throne and "look
pretty" is an entirely foreign idea to the Word of God. Kingship
and the throne in the Scriptures are symbols of service, not of
self-fulfillment or self-glory. To come to the throne of God
requires total commitment to Him, absolute obedience, and
spiritual character. There is no substitute. Spiritual character is
certainly not produced quickly or easily.

We do not know the kind of service that will be rendered in
the ages to come, but we do know the spiritual character that
alone qualifies us to reign with Him. Here we return to Jacob.
Through the things which he suffered, the Lord made him "a
prince of God." If we have understood anything of what I have
written about Jabbok, the wrestling of God with Jacob and
Jacob with God, we know that it cost God so much and Jacob
also! Coming to reign with Christ will cost us our self-
centeredness. There is no other way.

When Jacob came to Jabbok he was alone. We cannot become
overcomers in a "second-hand" or "third-hand" manner. It is not
possible to hide within the experience of others, as if one can join
a club of overcomers. We have to have our own direct and
personal dealings with the Lord. For this reason Jacob had to be
"alone." We have to know and to follow the Master ourselves.
This is an essential part of overcoming.

The Lord's purpose for Jacob that he should be
the head

The Lord declared, as I have mentioned a number of times,

> And the LORD will make thee the head, and not the tail; and
> thou shalt be above only, and thou shalt not be beneath; if

thou shalt hearken unto the commandments of the LORD thy
God, which I command thee this day, to observe and to do
them, and shalt not turn aside from any of the words which I
command you this day, to the right hand or to the left, to go
after other gods to serve them.

(Deut. 28:13–14)

The Lord's purpose for Jacob (and his seed) had been from the
beginning that he should be the head and not the tail, that he
should be above only and not beneath. We should note "above
only." It took the Lord long years to bring Jacob to that
position. By his nature Jacob tried many times to be the head
and not the tail, to be above and not beneath. However, as
always with that which originates in our unbroken self-life,
it only accentuated the emptiness, the restlessness, and the
unhappiness in him. There was no real fulfillment. After
the Lord dealt with Jacob, the Spirit of God produced the kind
of character that can do no other but rule. From that point and
onwards, Jacob's life and character impacted everybody.

Made to sit with Christ in heavenly places

The apostle Paul wrote that God has "raised us up with him,
and made us to sit with him in the heavenly places, in Christ
Jesus" (Eph. 2:6). This is the New Testament version of
Deuteronomy 28:13–14. Only the Spirit of God can reveal the
position that we have in the Messiah, so that it becomes our
practical experience. Please note carefully that this is the
present position of the child of God, whether we feel it or not!
Secondly, note that God has made us *to sit* with the Messiah in
the heavenly places.

It is the absolute victory of the Lord Jesus that we are to
confess in the conflict on earth! He has won! It is the same truth
relating to warfare described in Ephesians 6:10–18. There we
are commanded to stand, withstand, and stand. Here we are

told that we have been made to sit with Him. In this conflict there are two positions vital for the victory of Christ to be experienced practically: sitting and standing. An academic knowledge of it will not suffice, for we will have the doctrine but not the reality. To know in experience what it is to sit with Christ in our present circumstances and condition is essential if we are to reign with Him in the future. It cannot remain theology; it must be experienced in practice.

If we are truly born again, we have been made alive together with Christ. If we have been raised together with Him, it is to a new creation, a new man, a new destiny, and a new power. If we are made to sit with Him in heavenly places, it is a new position that we have been given. We are "in Christ." This little phrase sums up everything about our salvation and our destiny. If only we who are the children of God knew what it means in experience "to sit with Him in heavenly places."

Years ago, a young man went to see the famous servant of God Dr F.B. Meyer. He had made an appointment, but when he arrived, F.B. Meyer had been held up by another engagement. The house mistress welcomed him and showed him into the doctor's study, saying, "Make yourself comfortable! The doctor will be with you shortly." The young man looked around the study, naturally interested in what was engaging the mind of this well-known servant of God. On the mantelpiece his eye was riveted by a motto engraved in gold on wood. It consisted of only two words: "Look Down." He thought to himself, "Surely that should be 'Look Up.'" At that point, Dr F.B. Meyer entered the study and said, "Oh, I see you are interested in that statement on my mantelpiece." "Yes," said the young man, "but everyone normally says we should 'look up,' not 'look down.'" Dr F.B. Meyer said, "It all depends on your position! If you are seated with Christ you look down on all of your problems and situations; if you are under them you look up." Reigning with Christ can only be reality if we are seated with Him in heavenly places, and only the Holy Spirit can reveal that as our position. For most of us, it is our position, but we do not know it in experience.

We see all of this exemplified in Jacob. He was now Israel, a prince of God and with God. For the rest of his life after Jabbok, he was to rule. He had, of course, tried to rule before that experience and, in one sense, had been successful. For example, he had succeeded with the stealing of the birthright, with the stealing of the blessing of the firstborn, and with the increasing of his own flock from Laban's flocks. He had influenced both people and circumstances. It was, however, wholly due to the energy of his own nature, and the ability he had to manipulate both people and situations to his own ends and for his own wellbeing. By the grace of God at Jabbok, he had been broken of his own power and enabled to have power with God. Now, as a result of this, he has power with men. The Lord invests divine power and authority in the lame Jacob. He rules with God and by God. The lame now begins to take the prey.

Taking the prey for God

The overcomer will always be involved in winning others. They will be in the forefront of the battle to take the prey from the enemy. Consider the words of Isaiah:

> Shall the prey be taken from the mighty, or the lawful captives be delivered? But thus saith the LORD, Even the captives of the mighty shall be taken away, and the prey of the terrible shall be delivered; for I will contend with him that contendeth with thee, and I will save thy children.
>
> (49:24–25)

The "lawful captives," to whom Isaiah refers, are those human beings who due to sin, disobedience, and transgression have become the rightful captives of the powers of darkness. We are surrounded by such prisoners. In fact, the whole unsaved world is a satanic prison-house. The Lord declares that these "captives of the mighty shall be taken away, and the prey of the terrible shall be delivered." This is the gospel entrusted to us. In other words, the Lord is in the business of liberating those who are destined for a lost eternity, even though they are "lawful captives."

The Lord even promises,

> I will contend with him that contendeth with thee, and I will save thy children.

Even the children of God's people who have become prey to demonic forces can be delivered and saved. Sometimes even true believers have, through compromise, disobedience, or sin become captives of the powers of evil and need the same powerful liberation. The promise of deliverance also includes them.

How and through whom are these captives of the mighty and the prey of the terrible to be delivered? It is obvious that only through the finished work of the Lord Jesus, the Messiah, can the lawful captives be redeemed, set free, and saved. On this basis alone, God has delivered us out of the power of darkness and transferred us into the kingdom of His dear Son (see Col. 1:13). We who have known His power to save and deliver have a solemn responsibility, for He commanded us to preach the gospel to the whole creation.

The prey of the terrible need to be delivered

Can any true believer disobey this command? Is it possible for those of us who have tasted His grace to ignore these captives? Apparently some manage to ignore them very well! In my estimation, it is impossible for children of God who walk with the Lord and are sensitive to Him, to live as if this world is not a prison-house of captives. The "prey of the terrible" need to be delivered. Do we not have a serious responsibility toward them, for which we will have to answer in the day to come?

There is a great need for men and women, saved by the atoning work of the Messiah, crippled by the cross, and empowered and equipped by the Holy Spirit, to be in this battle. The Lord could do this alone but He has chosen to do it through human vessels. Only the lame can take this prey! I believe this is one of the great needs of the present hour.

The weapons of our warfare

The apostle Paul writing to the Corinthians declares,

> For though we walk in the flesh, we do not war according to the flesh (for the weapons of our warfare are not of the flesh, but mighty before God to the casting down of strongholds), casting down imaginations, and every high thing that is exalted against the knowledge of God, and bringing every thought into captivity to the obedience of Christ . . .
>
> (2 Cor. 10:3–5)

From Paul's words we understand that it is not only people who are captives, taken prey by the devil, but human situations, circumstances, and attitudes as well. He speaks of these strongholds as imaginations, high things exalted against the knowledge of God, and thoughts that are not obedient to Christ. All who are in the work of God, and seeking to serve the Lord, know only too well situations where the powers of darkness invade the work and service of God, creating strongholds as a result. The work of the gospel and the building up of the church can then be paralyzed.

Are there not often situations too in the fellowship of God's people, in our families, in our homes, in our relationships, and in our businesses that are strongholds of the evil one? The problems these satanic situations create appear to be seemingly

immovable, insoluble, and invincible! On many occasions they
become a "power house" for trouble in the life and service of
God's people. When demonically inspired, they become a
veritable fortress of Satan to demoralize and defeat the children
of God.

However, there is no need to fear these fortresses of
darkness, as if nothing can be done about them. Through the
weapons with which we can be equipped by the Holy Spirit
from the Word of God, the most powerful and seemingly
invincible strongholds can be broken up and cast down!

Paul declares that these weapons of our warfare are "mighty
before God". It is of great importance that we should understand this phrase. It is variously translated: "mighty through
God" (KJV); "divinely powerful" (NASB); "powerful according
to God" (JND). The practical point is that only in the presence of
God Himself, and under His government, can these weapons be
operative. Then these strongholds can be destroyed, even when
they are satanic and demonic.

Spiritual warfare is not a game! It is serious. We need to use
the right weapons for the right battle; otherwise we will suffer
casualties and even defeat. For this reason, it needs to be
underlined in an emphatic manner that we can only experience
spiritual success in warfare when we operate these weapons
in the presence of God. It has to be under His leading and in
fellowship with other believers. When those conditions are met,
we will experience the powerful operation of these weapons,
resulting in the throwing down of enemy strong points.

Where, however, are there believers who together know
how to handle these spiritual weapons? Where are the good
soldiers of the Messiah Jesus, who as in an army, under
command and bound together, are able to war the good
warfare? In this matter we return to overcoming, for this warfare
is part of our training. It should be obvious that when we speak
of the lame taking *the prey*, we are speaking of spiritual conflict
and strife.

Put on the whole armor of God

It is in another letter of the apostle Paul that we have a vital commentary on this question. Writing to the Ephesians he says,

> Finally, be strong in the Lord, and in the strength of his might. Put on the whole armor of God, that ye may be able to stand against the wiles of the devil. For our wrestling is not against flesh and blood, but against the principalities, against the powers, against the world rulers of this darkness, against the spiritual hosts of wickedness in the heavenly places. Wherefore take up the whole armor of God, that ye may be able to withstand in the evil day, and, having done all, to stand. Stand therefore ...
>
> (Eph. 6:10–14)

We should carefully note how the apostle concludes the most complete revelation and exposition of the eternal purpose of God in the New Testament. There are many important, even essential things he could have emphasized as absolutely necessary if the work of the Lord was to prosper and be fulfilled. Instead, he takes this single matter and emphasizes the all-important need of being covered in the Messiah. He speaks of the need of being "strong in the Lord, and in the strength of His might"; of putting on the "whole armor of God" and thus winning the battle. When Paul speaks of armor, he is speaking of Christ. In the Messiah, the soldiers of Christ have complete covering, security, and protection. However fierce the onslaught of the enemy may be, they are absolutely safe and would be enabled to see the purpose of God fulfilled in their day.

The apostle is describing the conditions in spiritual warfare. He speaks of the stratagems of the devil (the wiles of the devil), of principalities and powers, of world rulers of darkness, of hosts of wicked spirits in the heavenlies, of war, and of "evil days." Paul clearly understood that if they did not stand in

Christ, they would lose much. He implores them to put on the whole armor of God, for only in this way would they "win the day." If they were not so covered, they could become captive to the enemy's stratagems and intentions. Indeed, they could become prey for the enemy. The history of the Church in the last 1,900 years illustrates this fact.

The way to win the battle – standing in Christ

On the one hand, he tells them "to stand against," "to withstand," "having done all, to stand," and "stand therefore..." This is surely the most extraordinary way to win battles! On the other hand, he declares that we are wrestling not against flesh and blood, but against the principalities, the powers, against the world rulers of this darkness, and against spiritual hosts of wickedness. In whom do we stand? In **Christ!** On what ground do we stand? On His finished work through which the devil has been brought to nought. For what do we stand? For God's purpose to be realized, in our day and generation. Why do we have to wrestle? For the simple reason that the powers of darkness and evil are seeking to take hold of us and defeat us! And how do we win the battle? By simply standing in Him.

It is worth recording that "standing," in this context, is a matter of maintaining a victory already won by the Messiah. The victory of the Lord Jesus is total and absolute. In the Messianic Psalm 110, significantly quoted a number of times in the New Testament, we read:

> The LORD saith unto my Lord, Sit thou at my right hand, until I make thine enemies thy footstool. The LORD will send forth the rod of thy strength out of Zion: rule thou in the midst of thine enemies. Thy people are free will offerings in the day of thy army, in the beauty of holiness"
>
> (Ps. 110:1–3 mg)

This Messianic prophecy was fulfilled in the person and work of the Lord Jesus. Everywhere in the New Testament, the victory of the Messiah, through His finished work at Calvary, is proclaimed.

We should note that the Messiah Jesus is seated at the Father's right hand. That is a position of rest, not conflict. The Father tells the Son to remain seated *until He makes* His enemies the footstool of His feet. He declares that He will send forth the rod of the Messiah's strength out of Zion and commands Him to rule in the midst of His enemies. From this, we understand that there is still much conflict and warfare; there are still many enemies. We who are on this earth are in this conflict and war.

It is of great significance that it is stated, in this connection, that, in the day of His army, God's people will be "free-will offerings," as volunteers. We should note that the Commander of the armies of heaven is not conscripting His children by force into His army. It is a "volunteer" army. We, however, whether we like it or not, are born into war and conflict and are called to be in His army. There is a vital link between the seated position of the Lord Jesus, the rod of His strength being sent forth out of Zion, His ruling in the midst of His enemies, and our being in His army.

We cannot stand against Satan, nor withstand in the evil day, unless first we have seen what it is to sit with Christ in heavenly places. His absolute victory, expressed in being seated with Him, is directly related to standing and withstanding until the forces of darkness yield in defeat.

Therefore, our responsibility, if we are in this army, is to proclaim the total victory of the Lord Jesus, won through His finished work, and to be the Father's instrument by which the enemies of the Messiah become His footstool. It is our job to maintain this victory by standing, withstanding, and, having done all, finally to stand (see Eph. 6:10–14).

If God has not dealt with us as He dealt with Jacob, we have a

Trojan Horse within us that will certainly ensure our defeat. Once again the truth we have seen in the life of Jacob is underlined. In overcoming there can be no compromise with our self-life. We have to come to our personal Jabbok. Then the lame can take the prey for God.

Chapter 12

DEATH WORKS IN US,
BUT LIFE IN YOU

Even after Jacob became Israel, his way was not easy. He buried his beloved Rachel, the one great love of his life. Throughout those years, his sons were a constant source of concern to him. He suffered much from their rivalries, their jealousies, and their intrigues. If that was not bad enough, there was worse: within the family, there was depravity, dishonesty, and even attempted murder. Jacob's way was not "a bed of roses," but *he* was different.

In the strength of his old life, he would have hardened himself against those situations and used his manipulative powers to change them, seeking to gain something out of them. Now he walked with God. He was infinitely more sensitive, and therefore what he saw around him brought pain to his heart. Through those years Jacob learned the nature of spiritual travail. He learned deeply and painfully as he saw his own nature in others, knowing that, as with himself, only God could change them. He could not be a partaker of their sinfulness but neither could he condemn them out of hand. He knew that they also had to come to their "Jabbok."

Somewhere at the heart of Jacob's being, the cross had touched his soul. That did not mean his soul had been eradicated, as if he had no soul. It meant that the *life* of his soul had been dislocated; his self-life was disabled. It would limp for the rest of his days. The result was that another Life, God's life, flooded him. Many of us have such unbroken souls that it is our *spirits* that "limp"! Only the cross can work so deeply in us that our *soul* limps and our spirit reigns! When this happens the Lord has His full way with us. He reigns in us. There is an ongoing experience of "the exceeding greatness of his power" (see Eph. 1:19). It is the power of the resurrection life of the Messiah flowing out as rivers of living water from the broken vessel.

Your spirit, soul, and body

The apostle Paul wrote to the Thessalonians,

> And the God of peace himself sanctify you wholly; and may your spirit and soul and body be preserved entire, without blame at the coming of our Lord Jesus Christ. Faithful is he that calleth you, who will also do it.
>
> (1 Thess. 5:23–24)

It is noteworthy that Paul defines the tripartite nature of the human being as spirit, soul, and body. He believes that all three elements are to be "preserved entire." There is no suggestion that the spirit and the soul are synonymous, or that the spirit is merely the noble aspect of the soul, or the soul the more base part of the spirit.

To be a spiritual person is to be governed by the Spirit of God in and through the human spirit. Simply stated, this means that our soul and body, our flesh, must come under the government of the Lord in our spirit. It is interesting that the scriptural order is "spirit, soul, and body," whereas we normally speak of "body, soul, and spirit." It is, of course, spoken spontaneously but reveals the priorities of fallen mankind. Whichever way we put it, the soul occupies the central position. This truth is important to our practical understanding of the matter. The soul is the seat of our will, of our reasoning, and of our emotions and feelings. The spirit is the only part of our being where the Spirit of God can take up residence. It is there that the Lord Jesus dwells through the Holy Spirit.

One must remember that Jacob was a different man after Jabbok. The face of God had shone on him. As I have already written, he could have described his experience there in a number of ways: for example, as "brokenness," "disabling," "lameness," "conversion," or "transformation." Instead he described it as the "face of God." The light of the knowledge of the glory of God in the face of Jesus, the Messiah, had shone into him and left its mark. He shone with the beauty of the Lord, but his soul was crippled.

The crippling of his soul did not mean that there was no appreciation in Jacob of beauty, no warmth of personality, no music in his being, no artistry or poetry in his soul. Jacob had not become "spiritual machinery" as a result of Jabbok. It simply meant that the Lord now governed his soul and his body from his spirit. Some Christians, when they begin to see the importance of this matter, try to suppress the soul. They then become unnatural and artificial people. The suppression of the soul is not God's answer. The only way our soul can be governed is when the Lord reveals Himself to us through His word and breaks its power.

The dividing of soul and spirit

The writer of the Hebrew letter also speaks of this matter,

> For the word of God is living, and active, and sharper than any two-edged sword, and piercing even to the dividing of soul and spirit, of both joints and marrow, and quick to discern the thoughts and intents of the heart.
>
> (4:12)

When man fell, he chose a different constitution from the one God had intended for him. Something terrible had happened. At that point his soul and spirit were merged. His human spirit became like an electric light-bulb alienated from its power source, its electrical socket, and unable therefore to give light. To all intents and purposes, it was as if his spirit was non-existent. The New Testament describes it as "dead" (e.g. Eph. 2:5). In fact, the human spirit can become a nest for evil spirits. As a result the fallen human being's soul became, with the body, the all-important factor in living. Our salvation restores the proper order.

The restoration of that order requires no little power. Through the Word of God, the Lord performs "spiritual surgery" and divides the soul from the spirit. These two have become so merged that they are like joints and marrow, virtually indivisible. If you understand the need for this essential operation, you will begin to understand the emphasis throughout this book. "Jabbok" is an absolute spiritual necessity for every child of God. There is no alternative and no substitute.

When this "spiritual surgery" has taken place, we know that which is the Lord in us, and that which is ourselves! It is the story of Jacob. Even as his hip was dislocated, causing him to limp for the rest of his life, so it will be with us in the division of soul and spirit. It is the beginning of overcoming. You cannot overcome if you do not know who you are and what you are, because there will always be the danger of deception, mixture, and divisiveness. For the first time you will experience the meaning of the word, "sanctify in your hearts Christ as Lord" (see 1 Pet. 3:15). "Sanctify" means "to set apart." The division of soul and spirit by the living and active Word of God has the same idea. It is Christ as Lord in your spirit, governing your soul, and body. When the soul and spirit are mixed together, Christ cannot be Lord practically, for we are always hearing the "voice" of our soul and believing that it is the voice of God! Spiritual surgery sets apart Christ as Lord in our spirit, separating Him and His voice from our own voice and inclinations.

If any man follow Me

Jacob's life after his experience at Jabbok, and until he went to be with the Lord, could be described by the words of the apostle Paul, "always bearing about in the body the dying of Jesus, that the life also of Jesus may be manifested in our body" (2 Cor. 4:10). Jacob became a picture, an example, of what the Lord wants every believer to be. The power of God's life in him, which turned him into both a mighty blessing and a humble worshiper, is an illustration of what the Lord would also work in us.

The Messiah Jesus declared,

> If any man would come after me, let him deny himself, and take up his cross, and follow me. For whosoever would save his life shall lose it; and whosoever shall lose his life for my sake and the gospel's shall save it.
>
> (Mark 8:34–35)

The fact that the Lord Jesus called the multitude together with His disciples to make this statement, reveals its vital importance. It is central to Christian life and service, and is an essential outcome of the gospel.

The Lord was preaching no cheap and easy gospel. He challenged all who would follow Him to surrender totally their self-life. What is that challenge? He speaks of "denying oneself," or giving up all right to one's self-life; of taking up the cross; and of losing one's life for His sake and the gospel's. This word "life" in the Greek is *psuche*, or "soul." It is our self-life. In these powerful words we have the challenge of the full gospel as the Lord Jesus preached it. It is a basic statement of the only way in which God's salvation can be fully experienced in the life and service of the believer. You can, of course, be converted without knowing this fullness of His salvation: many remain converts and never become disciples.

In a day when our "rights" are continuously defined and asserted, it comes as an uncomfortable shock to hear what the Lord said. For many modern Christians, it is an unpalatable truth which they find easier to ignore. What did He mean when He spoke of "taking up his cross"? In what way are we to be involved with the cross? It is the apostle Paul who explained it when he testified, "I am crucified with Christ, nevertheless I live, yet not I . . . " (Gal. 2:20 ĸjv). We should note that rarely, if ever, did a man sentenced to death carry the whole cross. He carried the cross beam to the place where the upright stake, often a tree trunk, was already in place. The meaning is simple. We must accept the sentence of death on our self-life. People and circumstances will crucify us! This was Jacob's experience with his family! It is worth noting that, in those days, a person sentenced to death had no more rights to assert!

We should also note that the Lord began this statement with "If any man would follow Me . . . " and ended it with "follow Me." Sometimes the matter of "taking up" one's cross is considered as an experience only for very special people; it is considered extraordinary, not normal. The Lord Jesus declares, however, that it lies at the heart of following Him. It is absolutely normal and necessary if you would be His disciple. In other words, it is impossible to follow the Lord Jesus and not deny one's self-life! No child of God can follow the Messiah very far before he or she finds the cross in their path. It is unavoidable. At that point you either preserve your self-life or you lose it.

Is it any wonder that such a teaching is ignored in our day? Yet it lies at the heart of a practical Christian life and service, at the heart of genuine church life and fellowship. It is the key to the fulfillment of God's eternal purpose, both for the individual and for the church. It is also the sad explanation for the lack of spiritual character amongst so many believers.

If it die, it beareth much fruit

In the Gospel of John the Lord Jesus returned to this matter in a deeper way:

> Verily, verily, I say unto you, Except a grain of wheat fall into the earth and die, it abideth by itself alone; but if it die, it beareth much fruit. He that loveth his life loseth it; and he that hateth his life in this world shall keep it unto life eternal. If any man serve me, let him follow me; and where I am, there shall also my servant be: if any man serve me, him will the Father honor.
>
> (John 12:24–26)

This honoring is not merely a question of respect but denotes that the Father will bring that servant of the Lord to the throne to reign with Christ. How can such a servant come to that position? Only by falling into the ground and dying! That statement is not ambiguous. It is starkly simple.

Jacob was a whole grain. On the one side, Jacob was handsome, attractive, and talented. On the other side, he was ugly, unattractive, and manipulative. Only when the whole unbroken grain that was Jacob fell into the ground and died, did Jacob bear much fruit.

Here we have the same word used as that recorded twice in Mark's Gospel. It is the word "life": "He that loveth his *life* loseth it," and "he that hateth his *life* . . ." It is again the Greek word *psuche*, "soul." We have another word translated "life" in the phrase "shall keep it unto *life* eternal." This is not *psuche*, "soul," but *zoe*, a word in the Bible which denotes not physical or biological life but spiritual life, the principle of life. He that loveth his soul or self-life shall lose it, and he that hates his soul or self-life in this world, shall keep it unto life eternal. Jacob re-discovered his soul, his self-life, under new management, the management of the Holy Spirit. It was now swallowed up by eternal life.

The deepest instinct in our being is to preserve ourselves. We seek always to protect, to further, or to fulfill ourselves. I have noticed that when children of God face the cross of Christ with its stark alternatives, either to preserve themselves intact or to surrender themselves in totality, those who surrender always come into a new experience of Christ's resurrection life. God gives back their soul, their self-life, under His government. Rivers of living water then flow out of their innermost being. The result is always fruitfulness. This is the story of Jacob after Jabbok.

Those Christians who have given up all right to themselves and have taken up their cross, become such warm and loving people. A spontaneity and originality often marks them. They have lost their self-life only to receive it back in new life. It has found its right place under the lordship of Jesus in their spirit. In other words, it is the lesson of Jacob's dislocated hip. It is the soul that is dislocated but life eternal is now shining through it. The end of this is bearing much fruit. Let that simple phrase sink deep within us: "*if* it die, it beareth much fruit."

Treasure in earthen vessels

In his second letter to the church in Corinth, the apostle Paul writes,

> But we have this treasure in earthen vessels, that the exceeding greatness of the power may be of God, and not from ourselves; we are pressed on every side, yet not straitened; perplexed, yet not unto despair; pursued, yet not forsaken; smitten down, yet not destroyed; always bearing about in the body the dying of Jesus, that the life also of Jesus may be manifested in our body.
>
> (4:7–10)

Here we have an amazing paradox! On the one hand, we have an earthen vessel, a clay pot, which has very little worth, and, on the other hand, we have treasure, which is valuable and precious. The extraordinary thing is that this valuable treasure has been placed in the clay pot. It is clear that Paul is writing of himself and us, for he says, "we have this treasure..." He explains this paradox by writing that God does this so that the "exceeding greatness of the power may be of God and not from ourselves." This is exemplified for us in the story of Jacob. After Jabbok it was the exceeding greatness of God's power that was manifest in him. It was clearly not from himself, for he was disabled and lame.

We should note that in this same context Paul has written of the light of the knowledge of the glory of God in the face of Jesus the Messiah (v. 6). In fact, it is the preceding sentence to the one in which he states, "but we have this treasure in earthen vessels." Note the word "but" at the beginning of this verse.

This testimony of the apostle is remarkable. If it was not in the Word of God, we would question whether Paul was not a candidate for deliverance. Carefully read what he writes:

> we are pressed on every side, yet not straitened; perplexed, yet not unto despair; pursued, yet not forsaken; smitten down, yet not destroyed...
>
> (vv. 8–9)

Note carefully, "pressed on every side ... perplexed ... pursued ... smitten down..." It hardly seems a normal living testimony, and certainly does not sound like "overcoming," unless we also note, "not straitened ... not unto despair ... not forsaken ... yet not destroyed..."

Paul describes this as "always bearing about in the body the dying of Jesus, that the life also of Jesus may be manifested in our body" (2 Cor. 4:10). It is the principle of resurrection life out of dying; power out of weakness; wholeness out of brokenness; summer out of winter; fruitfulness out of pruning; exaltation out of humbling. It is simply Israel out of Jacob.

In the same letter Paul writes that the Lord said to him, "My grace is sufficient for thee: for my power is made perfect in weakness" (2 Cor. 12:9a). Normally we would never associate power with weakness, and would never think of them as belonging to one another. God, however, declares that His power is made perfect in weakness. It comes to its full development in our brokenness. Paul saw this truth so deeply and experienced it so powerfully that he writes: "Most gladly therefore will I rather glory in my weaknesses, that the power of Christ may rest upon me" (v. 9b). It is worth noting that the Greek for "rest upon me" is "spread a tabernacle over me." Only when we are disabled like Jacob can the power of God tabernacle upon us, or dwell upon us.

This is the paradox of Christian life and service! On the one hand, it is the bearing about in the body the dying of Jesus and, on the other, the life of Jesus being manifested in our bodies. The apostle summed it up in one pregnant sentence:

> So then death worketh in us, but life in you.
>
> (2 Cor. 4:12)

There could be no clearer interpretation of the principle of lameness.

Chapter 13

JACOB AND MODERN ISRAEL

And So All Israel Shall Be Saved

God has forever given to His redeemed people the name of Jacob and of Israel. Upon that matter there can be little discussion, for even the most superficial reading of the Bible reveals it. The preceding chapters of this book have dwelt upon the many lessons which the redeemed can learn from the life of Jacob. In particular, we have emphasized the fact that it is the persevering love and grace of God that changes a Jacob into an Israel. For those who belong to the Lord, the lessons to be learned through Jacob are therefore full of comfort and encouragement.

Can we see, however, any hope for the physical seed of Jacob in his story? Has God still a purpose for the Jewish people, or has He totally rejected them? Are we to consider the recreation of the state of Israel in 1948 and the return of Jerusalem in its entirety to the Jewish people in 1967 as prophetic milestones, or are they merely political accidents in history that have led to much unnecessary suffering, turmoil, and war?

It is at this point that we enter into a subject of much heated debate and controversy amongst Christians. There are those who dogmatically assert that God has finished with the Jewish people. They teach that the Jews, the physical seed of Abraham and Jacob, were only a stepping-stone to the Church in which all the prophecies have been entirely fulfilled.

Altogether apart from the many prophecies in the Old Testament, which undoubtedly point to a fulfillment beyond the return from the Babylonian exile (circa fifth century BC), there are clear and unequivocal New Testament references.

I would not have you ignorant of this mystery

Can the plain words written by the apostle Paul in the Roman letter be misunderstood?

> For I would not, brethren, have you ignorant of this mystery, lest ye be wise in your own conceits, that a hardening in part hath befallen Israel, until the fulness of the Gentiles be come in; and so all Israel shall be saved: even as it is written, There shall come out of Zion the Deliverer; He shall turn away ungodliness from Jacob: And this is my covenant unto them, When I shall take away their sins.
>
> (Rom. 11:25–27)

Who is this *Israel*? It cannot be the Church! At present, by His grace, we are in the process of the full number of the Gentiles being brought into the true Church of God. Furthermore, it speaks of an Israel that has been hardened in part. A careful reading of these chapters 9–11 reveals that this is the physical *Israel* awaiting her final salvation.

It is even more remarkable to note that which the apostle goes on to write:

> As touching the gospel, they are enemies for your sake; but as touching the election, they are beloved for the fathers' sake. For the gifts and the calling of God are not repented of [irrevocable].
>
> (Rom. 11:28–29; cf. NASB)

The nation and people who are described in these three chapters as "disobedient," "gainsaying," "hardened," "blind," "deaf," "fallen," "lost," "cast away," "broken off," "unbelieving," and "enemies of the gospel" are the same nation of whom the Lord declares that their gifts and their calling have not been cancelled or revoked. Indeed, He says that as touching the election, they are beloved of Him for the patriarchs' sake.

It is not an accident that the Apostle writes of this matter as a "mystery" and states that he would not have them ignorant of it. When Paul uses the word "mystery," he is not meaning a matter totally and forever beyond us. He was borrowing a term from the Greek Mystery cults of his day, the new members of which were "initiated" into the secrets connected with those cults. In other words, the understanding of the mystery or secret of Israel is the birthright of every born-again believer! The Holy Spirit has to reveal it. The only condition is child-like humility.

It is no accident that this explanation of the history of the physical seed of Jacob in these last 1,900 years is found within the greatest exposition of the gospel in the Bible. So often, the three chapters that deal with this matter are either bypassed as unimportant or viewed as "hyper-theology" pertaining to the difficult matter of the predestination of the Church. In practice, for many believers, the Roman letter consists of only the first eight chapters. In fact, it is sometimes stated that, with his appeal in Romans 12:1, the apostle "returns" to his "original" theme, Romans 9–11 being considered a parenthesis. However, that is to miss the profound significance of these three chapters.

By their fall, salvation is come unto the Gentiles

The original purpose of God in choosing Abraham, and thus the Jews, was that, in his seed, all the nations of the earth would be blessed. This divine purpose was fulfilled not through the success of the Jewish people but, by the grace of God, through their failure. Thus the inspired statement of Paul,

> by their fall, salvation is come unto the Gentiles, to provoke them to jealousy. Now if their fall is the riches of the world, and their loss the riches of the Gentiles; how much more their fulness?
>
> (Rom. 11:11–12)

They were ordained to become the vehicle by which the revelation of God, the Word of God, the Messiah of God, and the salvation of God, came to the world. As the Lord Jesus declared, "salvation is from the Jews" (John 4:22; cf. Rom. 9:4–5). That gospel of the salvation of God, so powerfully expounded in the Roman letter, has now come to the ends of the earth. When the full number of the Gentiles to be saved is coming to completion, the Lord will melt the hardening in part that has befallen Israel – with the most powerful and glorious consequences.

> For as ye [the Gentiles] in time past were disobedient to God, but now have obtained mercy by their [the Jews'] disobedience, even so have these [the Jews] also now been disobedient, that by the mercy shown to you [the Gentiles], they also may now obtain mercy. For God hath shut up all unto disobedience, that he might have mercy upon all.
>
> (Rom. 11:30–32)

The whole redeemed family of God will have been saved to sin no more. So stunning is the impact of this revelation that the apostle can hardly express it in words:

> O the depth of the riches both of the wisdom and the knowledge of God! how unsearchable are his judgments, and

his ways past tracing out! For who hath known the mind of the
Lord? or who hath been his counsellor? or who hath first given
to him, and it shall be recompensed unto him again? For of
him, and through him, and unto him, are all things. To him be
the glory forever. Amen.

(Rom. 11:33–36)

I could wish that I were accursed . . .

The fact that Paul, in this exposition of the gospel, felt unable to
leave what he had written without dealing with the whole issue
of the Jewish people is in itself striking. It was not some pathetic
nationalism in his soul that compelled him to take up the
subject – it was the Spirit of God within him. So powerful was
the great sorrow and unceasing pain in his heart for the Jewish
people that he used words that have been the cause of much
discussion over the years. He expressed the wish that he could
be "accursed" or "anathematized" from the Messiah Jesus for
his brothers' sake, his kinsman according to the flesh, whom he
calls "Israelis." He could have used no stronger word. Are we
to consider this expression of his burden as merely personal,
emotional, and off-centre, or are we to understand its source as
the very heart of God in Paul? If the source of this consuming
burden in him was in God, then these three chapters have
tremendous significance for the Church, for the work of God,
and for our understanding of history and of the final events of
the age.

He shall turn away ungodliness from Jacob

It is instructive to note that the Spirit of God inspired the
apostle to quote a prophecy in Isaiah 59:20 from the Greek
translation of the original Hebrew made in the fourth century
BC, the Septuagint (LXX). (This version, of course, at that time
was the normal version used by the Church outside of Israel.)

There shall come out of Zion the Deliverer; He shall turn away ungodliness from Jacob . . .

(Rom. 11:26)

The original Hebrew reads a little differently,

And a Redeemer will come to Zion, and unto them that turn from transgression in Jacob, saith the LORD.

In my estimation the change between the Hebrew and the Greek is of very great significance. The Redeemer did come to Zion; it was the Messiah, the Lord Jesus. He did come to those "that turn[ed] from transgression"; that was the early Church, in its first years totally Jewish. The promised Deliverer coming out of Zion is still the Redeemer who first came to Calvary. He will deliver Jacob by the finished work of redemption which He wrought on the cross. It will be the completion of the purpose that began to be fulfilled at Pentecost.

A prophetic enactment?

It is noteworthy that the Greek of the LXX states that the Deliverer, the Messiah, by the Holy Spirit will *turn away* ungodliness from Jacob. This has the most uncanny similarity to Jabbok: Jacob transformed into Israel. Is it therefore fanciful to recognize the possibility, even the probability, that the changing of Jacob into Israel at Jabbok is a prophetic enactment of what will happen with the physical seed of Jacob? In Romans 11:26 we read, "so all Israel shall be saved," and also, "He shall turn away ungodliness from Jacob." In this one verse we have both "Israel" and "Jacob"; and, even more significantly, Israel is saved when ungodliness is turned away from Jacob.

If this is, as I believe, a prophetic insight into the last events of this age, then we should expect to see the main features of what happened at Jabbok re-enacted. The essential elements would be: the absolute aloneness of Jacob; the recognition of the insolubility of his problem (he could neither go back nor could he go forward); the fear that gripped and possessed him; the deep, almost hidden, sense of divine destiny and calling; the realization that he was hopeless and not what he should be; and the desperation that led him to refuse to let the heavenly visitor go. As it was personally with Jacob, so it will be with the Jewish people.

Those who have eyes to see must surely recognize that most, if not all, of these features are present in modern Israel at this point in history. When the divinely appointed time comes, it will not only be a new birth, but a transformation into the likeness of the Messiah. It will be Jacob into Israel. Once again, the determining factors are the undying, persevering love and mercy of God, divine election, and an appointment that God Himself has made and will keep.

The restoration of the kingdom to Israel

In Acts 1:6 we have a further reference to Israel in the question that the disciples asked the risen Lord: "Lord, dost thou at this time restore the kingdom to Israel?" The fact that for over forty days the Lord Jesus had spoken to His disciples about "the things concerning the kingdom of God" (see Acts 1:3), helps us to understand why they asked this question of Him.

It is sometimes stated that these disciples were so blinded and bound by their nationalism that when He was about to ascend to the right hand of God, the only question in their minds concerned the nation of Israel. It is then pointed out that the Lord never mentioned Israel, only saying,

> ye shall receive power, when the Holy Spirit is come upon you: and ye shall be my witnesses both in Jerusalem, and in all Judaea and Samaria, and unto the uttermost part of the earth.
>
> (Acts 1:8)

The idea in this interpretation is that the Lord Jesus essentially dismissed the question of Israel, as if the work of the Spirit would begin in Jerusalem, advance to Judea and Samaria, reach the ends of the earth, and never return! National Israel is then seen as an anachronism, a relic relating only to past history. However, it is noteworthy that the disciples did not ask, "Will You restore the kingdom to Israel?" but "Will You *at this time* restore the kingdom to Israel?" That is a very different question!

Times and seasons within God's authority

It is important to recognize that, in answering it, the Lord said,

> It is not for you to know times or seasons, which the Father hath set within his own authority. But ye shall receive power...

There are times and seasons for the restoration of the kingdom to Israel. The disciples were not to be focused on that matter, for they had a work to do beginning in Jerusalem and reaching to the ends of the earth. In speaking about the matters concerning the kingdom of God over those forty days, the Lord Jesus must have mentioned Israel's restoration a number of times for the disciples to have specifically questioned Him as to whether that time had arrived. Are we not in those times and seasons? The gospel has indeed gone to the ends of the earth, although there is still more work to be done. It is also true that for the first time in some one thousand nine hundred years a Jewish state has arisen within the original promised land; and in 1967 Jerusalem became the capital of that state. Surely this is evidence that we have finally arrived at these times and seasons of which the Messiah spoke. The whole world now recognizes that the situation in the Middle East, and in particular as relating to Israel, is not only dangerous but could involve the world in war! This fact highlights the fulfillment of God's prophetic word. Who would believe that a little state of seven million people, in a postage stamp of territory, surrounded by a sea of Islam, could be so important? This world importance is even more remarkable when one remembers that there has not been a Jewish state for some 2,000 years, and that Jerusalem has been a "backwater" throughout that time. Yet Zechariah the prophet has warned us that both the recreated Jewish state, and Jerusalem as its capital, would cause world conflict (see Zech. 12–14).

Until the times of the Gentiles be fulfilled

The words of the Lord Jesus as recorded in Luke 21:24 have serious significance for those who live in the end times. He said, "and Jerusalem shall be trodden down of the Gentiles, until the times of the Gentiles be fulfilled." It is clear that He made the status of Jerusalem the key to any understanding of the last phase of world history. We note that He spoke of Jerusalem being "trodden down of the Gentiles, *until* the times of the Gentiles be fulfilled" (my emphasis). In other words, whilst Jerusalem was under a non-Jewish government and administration, the times of the Gentiles were still in force. The moment, however, Jerusalem returned to Jewish government, the times of the Gentiles would be concluded. On 7 June 1967, an incredible miracle took place and Jerusalem in its entirety came back to the Jews. For the last forty years it has remained fully in Jewish hands as the capital of Israel. Anyone who has visited Jerusalem in these last years must have noticed its overall Jewish character. It is everywhere apparent. This has to be the most powerful sign since Calvary and Pentecost. From the biblical viewpoint, it marks a sea change in the course of world history!

Dr Martyn Lloyd-Jones, that great expositor of the Word of God and uncompromising stalwart of the truth of God, in an interview with Dr Carl Henry, founding editor of *Christianity*

Today, said, "To me, 1967, the year that the Jews occupied all of Jerusalem, was very crucial. Luke 21:24 is one of the most significant prophetic verses: *'Jerusalem,'* it reads, *'shall be trodden down of the Gentiles until the time of the Gentiles be fulfilled.'* It seems to me that took place in 1967 – something crucially important that has not happened for 2,000 years. Luke 21:24 is one fixed point, but I am equally impressed by Romans 11, which speaks of a great spiritual return of the Jews before the end of time."

Jerusalem will yet see much suffering and shed many more tears, but the fact remains that she is today larger, more influential, more vibrant, and probably more beautiful than she has been in her long 4,000 years of history. Today she remains the divine sign that she commenced to be when King David captured her and made her his capital. From that time, she has been a living sign that the Word of God is accurate, trustworthy, and relevant. The fact that she is now the capital of Israel, betokens that the times of the Gentiles, that long period in world history, is over; and the last phase of world history has begun. That phase will end with the coming again of the Messiah. Is it therefore any wonder that Jerusalem is the focal point of strife, conflict, and war? Her status as Israel's capital will be contested even more ferociously as we progress to the end of the age. The Word of God, however, stands sure. When all is over, Jerusalem shall stand where Jerusalem ever stood (see Zech. 12:6).

Loved with everlasting love

It has already been pointed out that there are many references in the Old Testament to the return of the exiles to the promised land, to the recreation of its fertility and ecology, to the rebuilding of its cities and towns, and to the recreation of the state of Israel.

It is often taught that all those prophecies were fulfilled in the return from the exile in the fifth century BC, and that therefore we should not look for any further fulfillment. However, a careful study of these prophecies would seriously challenge that conclusion. If we believe in the full authority and inspiration of the Bible, such a view will leave us confused and with many questions. How accurate is God's Word? How much in the Old Testament is "poetic exaggeration"? Indeed, is the Old Testament trustworthy? Is it even relevant in the twenty-first century?

Let us consider one example of such a prophecy: Jeremiah 31. It is interesting to note that the names of Jacob and of Israel are repeated many times within it. Even the name of Rachel is mentioned. If this incredible prophecy was exhaustively fulfilled in the return from Babylon, as many teach, we have a serious problem. In predicting the return of the exiles to the promised land, Jeremiah specifically mentions the mountains of Samaria:

> Again shalt thou plant vineyards upon the mountains of Samaria; the planters shall plant, and shall enjoy the fruit thereof.
>
> (Jer. 31:5)

Jews have no dealings with Samaritans

We know that when the Jews returned to the land in the fifth century BC, they resettled Jerusalem, Hebron, Bethlehem, the Galilee, and most of the land; but *they did not* resettle Samaria. In fact, an intense bitterness developed between the Samaritans and the Jews that lasted for centuries, and had not lost its intensity in the time of Christ. Most Christians will recall the meeting between the Lord Jesus and the Samaritan woman recorded in John 4, and her words, "How is it that thou, being a Jew, askest drink of me, who am a Samaritan woman?"; and the comment by John, "For Jews have no dealings with

Samaritans." The fact is simple: Samaria was *not* recolonized in the return from the exile in Babylon.

The time frame for the fulfillment of this prophecy

Are we to believe that God's prophetic word could be so inaccurate? Indeed, if there is such a glaring inaccuracy at the heart of this prophecy, is it possible to trust the rest of it? However, if this reference to Samaria is an indication of the time frame when this prophecy would be fulfilled, it becomes a strong encouragement to trust in the Word of God. Only in this generation has Samaria once again been settled by Jews. Whatever may be the political and humanitarian view of it, much of the present conflict in the Middle East is focused on Judea and Samaria. It is even more interesting that these settlers have planted vineyards, and some of their wines have won prestigious awards. What makes this fact so impressive is that for at least a thousand years wine was not even allowed to be produced commercially in Samaria. This was due to the Islamic ban on alcohol in all areas that they governed. Far from being inaccurate, this prophetic word of Jeremiah has been precisely fulfilled in our day.

From the uttermost parts of the earth

Moreover, for those who have watched either films or videos of the returning exiles, whether survivors of the Holocaust from Europe, or from the countries of North Africa and the Middle East, or from Ethiopia, the description that the Lord gives of them is incredibly accurate:

> For thus saith the LORD, sing with gladness for Jacob, and shout for the chief of the nations; publish ye, praise ye, and say, O Lord, save thy people, the remnant of Israel. Behold, I will bring them from the north country, and gather

them from the uttermost parts of the earth, and with them the blind and the lame, the woman with child and her that travaileth with child together: a great company shall they return hither. They shall come with weeping; and with supplications will I lead them . . .

(Jer. 31:7–9)

The Lord predicts the scattered exiles will come from "the uttermost parts of the earth." Is this latter phrase to be understood as "poetic exaggeration," or is it an indication that this prophecy was not fulfilled in the return from Babylon? In fact, at that time they returned almost completely from the east. That can hardly be described as "the uttermost parts of the earth." However, it accurately and precisely describes the modern return of the Jewish exiles. They have come from nearly one hundred countries: for example, from the south: from South Africa, the Argentine, Australia, and New Zealand; from the east: from Persia, Iraq, Afghanistan, China, India, and Singapore; from the west: from Great Britain, Europe, the United States, and Canada; and from the north. It is interesting that the Spirit of God singles out "the north country." Babylon was, of course, east of the promised land. It is true that the major trade routes between Babylon and Israel entered the land from the north; but that hardly fits the prophecy. If, however, it is a reference to the recent huge immigration of at least one million Russian Jews, it is absolutely accurate. The Russian Jewish influx has brought with it much brilliance in the arts, in medicine, and in science, and also some thorny problems.

A solemn and powerful sign to the nations

This gathering of the exiles is, the Lord declares, a solemn and powerful sign to the nations of the world; and we are commanded to make it known.

> Hear the word of the LORD, O ye nations, and declare it in the
> isles afar off; and say, He that scattered Israel will gather him,
> and keep him, as a shepherd doth his flock.
>
> (Jer. 31:10)

Twice the Lord scattered them, and twice He has regathered
them. Israel is the only instance, in the history of the world, of a
nation twice exiled and twice brought back to its original
territory. In the first instance, they were exiled for fifty years
(seventy years' captivity, fifty years' exile) to approximately
1,000 miles or 1,600 kilometers east of the land of Israel. In the
second instance, they were exiled for approximately 1,900 years
into nearly every part of the earth, and returned from nearly
one hundred different countries. Israel is the only modern
nation that has arisen in its original homeland after an absence
from it of almost two millennia.

Is this to be explained by Jewish ingenuity, wealth, and
cunning, or is it the hand of God? If it is the hand of God, the
undying hatred and the continuous conflict are to be explained:
its source is to be found in Satan, whether in the unsaved world,
in the Church, or amongst believers.

Kept as a shepherd keeps his flock

Furthermore, it is not only the Lord's scattering and gathering
of Israel that is miraculous – it is also His declaration that He
will "keep him, as a shepherd doth his flock." In the fifty-nine
years of Israel's modern history, she has known eight wars and
in all of them the Lord has kept her. Israel is so small that she
has only to lose one major battle and she would be finished. To
these eight wars, we could add a ninth: the intifada, in which
thousands of both Israelis and Palestinians have lost their lives
or have been permanently disabled. Yasser Arafat launched it
when he rejected the offer made by Ehud Barak, Israel's prime
minister, at Camp David, in the USA, in July 2000. Barak had

offered some 96–98 percent of the West Bank, half of Jerusalem, and permanent sovereignty over the Temple Mount. The fact that Arafat refused the offer is evidence that the Islamic nations around Israel still believe that they should be able to liquidate little Israel, and will settle for nothing less. We can therefore expect many more attempts.

It is then of great encouragement and comfort to those who pray for Israel that the Lord Himself has given a promise that He who gathered Israel would keep him as a shepherd does his flock. For those who have watched the care with which shepherds tend and guard their flocks, it is a stirring and comforting promise.

The growing hostility to Israel and her isolation by the world in general is alarming, and portends much more serious conflict to come. Indeed, as I have already written, the prophet Zechariah has predicted this fact (see Zech. 12). It is an almost inescapable conclusion that we are watching a rerun of the events in the last century which resulted in the Holocaust and the liquidation of at least six million Jews. Out of that horror, Israel was born.

It now appears that the powers of darkness are mobilizing their forces again for one last attempt to frustrate the purpose of God, not only for Israel but also for the true Church. Out of that conflict and tribulation will come the salvation of Israel.

Israel is a divine sign

If the scattering of Israel was a divine sign to the nations, so is the gathering and security of Israel. As far as God and the fulfillment of His word and purpose is concerned, it is of no practical consequence to Him if the world is blind to it. The nations may be in uproar, but He that sits in the heavens laughs. He will still fulfill His purpose. It is, however, of very real and grave consequence for those nations that meddle with His purpose, be they small or large. The manner in which they touch this divine sign, determines the manner in which the Lord will deal with them.

The Lord makes a solemn promise in this prophecy concerning the seed of Israel:

> Thus saith the LORD, who giveth the sun for a light by day and the ordinances of the moon and of the stars for a light by night, who stirreth up the sea so that the waves thereof roar; the LORD of hosts is his name: If these ordinances depart from before me, saith the LORD, then the seed of Israel also shall cease from being a nation before me for ever.
>
> (Jer. 31:35–36)

He promises that so long as there is a sun and a moon and stars and the seas, the seed of Israel will never disappear as a nation. It would be difficult to misunderstand this promise, for it is so clear. Whilst there is a night and a day, and seasons, Israel will remain as a nation. It is therefore hard to understand those who teach that God has finished with Israel as a nation! Of course it can be spiritualized: the Church is that nation, and the words of the apostle Peter are often used to confirm this view (see 1 Pet. 2:9–10).

It is, however, of great importance to note the manner in which Jeremiah continues in verse 37:

> Thus saith the LORD: If heaven above can be measured, and the foundations of the earth searched out beneath, then will I also cast off all the seed of Israel for all that they have done, saith the LORD.

This is precisely what is erroneously but often taught, that God has rejected the Jewish people because of what they have done. The fact that the Jewish people have survived through thousands of years as a distinct people, although dispersed throughout the earth, is surely evidence that God has kept this promise. No other nation similarly dispersed has survived the ravages of time – only the Jews. Nations more powerful and with greater populations have been assimilated into others, and have disappeared. The Jewish people have not only survived as a distinct people, but the world has witnessed the recreation of their statehood. Is this to be considered an accident or a coincidence, or is it the evidence of the faithfulness of God to His word and the expression of His everlasting love?

The key: the everlasting love of God

The key to the survival of the Jews is indeed to be found in the cry from the heart of God,

> I have loved thee with an everlasting love: therefore with lovingkindness have I drawn thee. Again will I build thee, and thou shalt be built, O virgin of Israel . . .
>
> (Jer. 31:3–4)

It is the undying, persevering love of God that is the key to Jewish history. In fact, the story of the Jewish people is a divine love story, and we have come to the last chapter, and almost the last paragraphs. Carefully note the words of the Lord, "therefore with lovingkindness have I drawn thee. Again will I build thee . . . " The Lord declares that the bringing back of the Jewish people, the recreation of their statehood, and the rebuilding of their national institutions are the consequence of His fathomless grace: "therefore with lovingkindness have I drawn thee." This grace, this lovingkindness, this *hesed*, underlies Jewish history and it will ultimately lead Israel to salvation.

It was the love of God that was the key to Jacob's life. The Lord would not let him go, but loved him in the end from Jacob into Israel. It will be the same with the Jewish people. When

David Ben Gurion, with other Jewish leaders, discussed and debated what they should call the state that was about to be born in 1948, a number of names were suggested. In the end, they settled on "Israel." It was surely prophetic.

Chapter 14

THE UNDYING LOVE AND GRACE OF GOD

From the beginning it was the purpose of God to change Jacob into Israel. It was a purpose full of divine glory. It was not some small, narrow purpose, but that which lies at the heart of human history and, above all, of divine history. In the preceding pages of this book, I have sought to cover the life of Jacob, its significance, and the lessons we can learn from it. In summing up these lessons, there are four major factors in his life and experience which finally need to be re-emphasized.

Jacob's problem was Jacob

The first factor which I have sought to define in this book was the source of Jacob's problem. It was Jacob himself! He was the problem in the realization and fulfillment of God's purpose for him. It was not that he did not have understanding of spiritual matters, or that he was not aware of spiritual realities. The fact that he valued the birthright and the blessing reveals that he had some spiritual understanding and awareness. That was not the problem. With Esau it *was* the problem! He had no understanding of such things. By this world's standards he would be accounted a fine man, but he lived only for the world; for the things of time and of sense. On the other hand, Jacob had a real desire for the things of God and placed a high value on everything concerning the Lord. His zeal and devotion for those eternal values are evident in his story.

Jacob's problem was also not a question of endurance. The fact that he had worked for seven years to win Rachel, reveals stamina and determination. His twenty years with his uncle Laban were not easy years, but he endured them with patience. Patience and endurance were not the problem with him. He did not lack determined commitment to the goals he set for himself. His problem was the strength of his natural character, and the uncontrollable and powerful self-will which energized him. Unwittingly, he was in bondage to himself and to his own opinions and concepts. His natural shrewdness and his business acumen insulated him against any doubts he might have had concerning himself. *Jacob's problem was Jacob.* It was the spontaneous strength of an unbroken self-life. That was the source which spawned all the deceit, the scheming, and the supplanting.

When the Lord chose Jacob, He chose a bundle of difficulties. In choosing him, He chose no small problem. With God, however, nothing is impossible! He never let go of him, and never gave up on him. The Lord was the only One Who could save Jacob from his sin, from Satan, from the world, and from *himself.* For this reason, on not a few occasions, God calls Himself the Redeemer of Jacob.

It is a fact of the deepest significance that the only names given corporately to the people of God are both the names of one single man. Those names are Jacob and Israel. Although I have repeatedly drawn attention to this point throughout this book, it is so important that it needs to be re-emphasized. God could have called His redeemed by the name of Abraham, or of Joseph, or of Moses, or even of Joshua. Instead, the name God chose to give to His own was *Jacob*, the one He redeems and saves; and *Israel*, the one He formed out of Jacob and transformed into a "prince of God."

Why does the Lord call those of us He saves and redeems "Jacob" and "Israel"? The answer is simple! In the same manner in which Jacob himself was *the* problem, we also are *the* problem! In fact, the Lord has as many problems as He has children! For this reason, the story of Jacob and the necessary and essential lessons we learn from him, are of such hope and comfort to us.

Unfortunately, like Jacob, we are generally unaware that we are the root of the trouble. We blame our problems on our circumstances, on our situations, on our genetic history, on our temperament, and nearly always on our relationships with other human beings; but never, or rarely, on ourselves. We are unaware that, like Jacob, we are the problem. It is not merely *in* you and me, it *is you and me.*

Sometimes it is stated that the problem is Christians who do not "see." We are told that they have little or no knowledge of God's Word, and little or no understanding of God's purpose. So often, however, it is the Christians who do "see" who are the problem. We seek to win others to Christ and, at the same time, by our conduct and behavior, we deter them from ever coming to the Lord. We recognize deeper spiritual truths and at the same time frustrate the fulfillment of those truths in ourselves or in others. We appreciate the things of God and at the same time compromise His work, opening it up to forces other than the Spirit of God. We have a zeal for the Lord's house and wreck the building of it. It is Jacob. That is the real problem. It is not that you and I are necessarily manipulators or supplanters, but it is the powerful and spontaneous strength of our nature which carries us along, and for which we have no answer, and over which we have no victory. It comes as a shock to us to recognize, as did Jacob, that our unbroken self-life is the complex and often intractable obstacle to the fulfillment of God's purpose and work in our lives and in the life of the church. The first lesson we learn from Jacob, therefore, is simple. We are *ourselves* the problem!

The path to glory lies through the cross

The second major factor is "Jabbok." If Jacob was to become Israel, a prince of God and a prince with God, there was no alternative to it. If the problem that Jacob presented was to be solved, Jabbok was the only answer. There Jacob, the problem, was transformed into Jacob, the one who blesses; into Jacob, the worshiper; and into Jacob, the overcomer. I have repeatedly stated this one truth in the pages of this book, that there was and is no alternative to Jabbok. I make no apology for the repetition of this vital lesson.

Jacob called his experience there *Peniel*, the face of God. This is the only way to understand Calvary. There on the cross, when the Lord Jesus became sin for us, our salvation was won. In the suffering face of the Messiah, we behold the face of God. It is there that the heart and mind of God is most fully revealed, and His character most clearly expressed.

It is also there that we died with Him; we were crucified with Him. That truth is not meant to be mere brokenness, devastation, or the losing of one's self-life; it is the face of God shining on His child, the presence of the Lord in powerful grace and fullness. One can always recognize a child of God who has had such an experience. They radiate light and love, even if they are unaware of it. The face of God has not only shone on them, it shines through them. There is an idea with some believers that to be crucified with Christ means that you must appear to be afflicted, broken, and cramped in style. I call this "the affliction syndrome." It is entirely false. It is religion! A genuine experience of Calvary means that we are saved and born of God; that is fundamental. It also means that if we go on to accept the sentence of death on our self-life, the brokenness that follows will be swallowed up by the outshining of His grace and power.

There is no way that God's children can truly serve Him, or follow Him, without the cross. It lies at the heart of our salvation. It also lies at the heart of the Christian life, of following Christ, of true service and worship, and of the house of God. Jacob is forever the illustration of this principle. You can be a child of God, recognizing all the truths of the gospel, and lead a defeated and empty Christian life. Like the children of Israel in the wilderness, for a lifetime you can journey in an endless cycle, always seemingly moving but never in fact arriving! Spiritually speaking, Jabbok is the crossing over from the wilderness into the promised land.

Calvary (or Jabbok) is the sentence of death on our self-life, that we should not trust in ourselves, but in God. The heart of the matter is the giving up of all right to ourselves and the breaking of our own natural strength and power. It is the taking up of the cross and following Christ, that we might experience the power and fullness of God. For Jacob, Jabbok was the face of God, the presence of God. It broke him and delivered him from the bondage and the barrenness of self-centeredness. There is also for us no other path. The way to glory lies through the cross, through Jabbok. This is the second major factor in the life of Jacob.

There is no overcoming without God-given faith

The third major factor in Jacob's life and experience is as simple as the first two factors. There can be no overcoming without God-given faith. The Lord Himself is the source of a life that wins; He is the power that changes us into His own likeness. God-given faith is the only means through which a saved human being can be united to God. It joins the child of God to the Lord as his or her life and power. Whatever begins with the Lord has all the possibilities of ending with the Lord; whereas that which does not begin with the Lord has no possibility of ending with the Lord. Living, working faith enables us to begin with the Lord, to grow in the Lord, and to end with the Lord!

It is for this reason that the crisis Jacob experienced at Jabbok was the deciding factor in his life. At that point, the Lord had brought Jacob to a genuine understanding of himself. He had seen himself with such clarity that he felt "undone." His whole life was in ruins, and he was in a state of hopelessness. At Jabbok there arose in his heart that which I have described as "the desperation of faith." It was that God-given faith which could not and would not let the Lord go. The fact of the matter is that deeper than all Jacob's self-life, and the messes into which he had brought himself, was this genuine and living faith. It was the same kind of faith that Peter possessed, even when he denied the Lord three times, and of which the Lord Jesus said, "I have prayed for thee, that thy faith fail not." It neither failed with Peter nor with Jacob! For when all seemed lost, and Jacob was desperate, the Lord appeared. It was that true and God-given faith, deeper than Jacob's twistedness, which wrestled with God and would not let Him go. Only the Lord could have made Himself weak enough for Jacob to defeat. That "defeat" which the Lord suffered, changed Jacob forever. Like a laser beam, it shone into Jacob's self-life, breaking it and bringing him to a new place of worship, of blessing, and of fullness. From that point and onwards, Jacob became the bondslave of the Lord.

Here then is the mystery of divine election and grace. We see in Jacob's experience the two truths that, with our finite minds, we find impossible to reconcile: the predestinating power of God to choose and the responsibility of man to will and to act. The Lord never let Jacob go, but arranged his circumstances and problems in such a manner that Jacob was *forced* both to will and to act. God had cornered him. It was the persistence and perseverance of God that gave rise to the persistence and perseverance of Jacob. It brought out that faith which was the gift of God in him. It had been obscured, almost buried, by his own self-will and self-assertiveness. When all was seemingly lost, the Lord wrestled with Jacob, and so provoked him that Jacob would not let him go. The transformation of Jacob into

Israel was a masterpiece of God's grace. It is also a supreme illustration of the fact that there can be no overcoming without God-given faith.

It is the same with us. The Lord never lets go of us, and never gives up on us. Patiently He puts up with us all the way through the course of our lives, until He loves us from Jacob into Israel. It is *the exercise* of this God-given faith which unites us to the Lord; which joins us to His power and His grace. From those who have been twisters and manipulators, bound in the prison house of their self-life, He produces princes of God. The sheer artistry of His grace is seen in the way He produces royal and eternal character out of human debris and rubbish; it is seen in the manner in which He produces sacrificial service out of empty, selfish, and self-centered lives. Only the Holy Spirit can take us from dust to glory. This is the third major factor in the life of Jacob.

The undying love and grace of God

The fourth major factor in the life and experience of Jacob is, in my estimation, the most important of all. In fact, it underlies the other three, giving rise to them. That factor is the undying love and grace of God. The Lord declared to the seed of Jacob:

> I have loved thee with an everlasting love: therefore with lovingkindness have I drawn thee.
>
> (Jer. 31:3; cf. vv. 4, 7, 11)

Whatever some may claim is the meaning of the Hebrew *olam*, translated by the English word "everlasting," here it means "everlasting"! The love of God for His own is infinite, exhaustless, and as long lasting as God Himself. It is the *only* explanation for Jacob. Without that strong, stern, and patient love, enduring and exhaustless in its quality, there would be no Jacob about whom to write.

Carefully note the manner in which the Lord continues: "therefore with lovingkindness have I drawn thee." The words are fathomless in their meaning. It was certainly the Lord who "drew" Jacob from his birth to his final moments on this earth, arranging all his circumstances, his situations, and even his thorny and seemingly insoluble problems. Moreover, it was with grace, with *hesed* – that persevering, loyal, overcoming, and merciful love – that the Lord drew him. It is that noteworthy Hebrew word which runs like a gold thread through the pages of this book! Without it there would be no story of Jacob to tell. "Everlasting love" and "lovingkindness," or grace, are divine twins, never to be separated.

In order to bring him to Jabbok, the Lord often used Jacob's natural self-centeredness, his unbroken self-life, and the muddles and messes which he had himself created. It was not only the good events and incidents which the Lord used, but also Jacob's bad experiences. Here we are face to face with the sternness of God's love and His inescapable and invincible grace. There is nothing "sugary" or sentimental in either His love or His grace. The Lord will go to any lengths to change us into His likeness and bring us to His goal.

It was God's abounding grace that drew Jacob ever onwards to the glory of God. The words of the apostle Peter in his first letter could be used as a commentary on the life of Jacob:

> And the God of all grace, who called you unto his eternal glory in Christ, after that ye have suffered a little while, shall himself perfect, establish, strengthen you.
>
> (1 Pet. 5:10)

It is the same with every Jacob whom the Lord saves. It is the God of all grace who will not let us go, but draws us ever onward toward the goal, to the prize of the high calling of God in Christ Jesus.

Chapter 15

THE GOD OF JACOB

The key to the life of Jacob from his birth to his death was not Jacob's persistence, or his recognition of the vital nature of divine things, important as they may have been. We discover the real key within the name which God uses of Himself some twenty-one times in the Bible: the God of Jacob. This name in particular radiates the faithfulness, the loyalty, and the mercy of God. More than any other name of God, it expresses the quality of His love and grace: it is inexhaustible and fathomless. There is no other way to understand Jacob. Here we discover the secret of the patient endurance of God with Jacob: it is His endless mercy and His unswerving faithfulness. We also discover the secret of the transformation of Jacob into Israel. It is the same undying love. In the final analysis, it is not Jacob's recognition of eternal values or his persistence that is the secret, but the God of Jacob. He is both the secret and the explanation of the triumph of Jacob.

How amazing is the fact that the Infinite and Holy God, who dwells in light unapproachable, links Himself intimately with Jacob, the sinner, the twister, naming Himself the God of Jacob. Sometimes the question is asked, "What's in a name?" In this name of God everything is crystallized: the whole purpose of God for Jacob and fallen man: his redemption, his deliverance, and his transformation.

Furthermore, the Lord refers to Himself at least five times as "the Mighty One of Jacob." Through Isaiah, for example, the Lord declares, "thou shalt know that I, the Lord, am thy Savior, and thy Redeemer, the Mighty One of Jacob" (Isa. 60:16). It can only be of immense comfort to those whom God has saved and redeemed to hear these words. The Lord could have called Himself the Mighty One of Abraham, the Mighty One of Moses, or the Mighty One of David. It would have been true and would have furnished us with much material for spiritual messages! It would, however, not have had the same message as the Mighty One of Jacob.

It is awe-inspiring to realize that the infinite power of God is placed wholly on the side of those whom He saves, poor and failing as they may be. His might and power far outweighs their weakness and frailty. The simple meaning of this is stunning. Like the irresistible current of an ocean, this might and power can carry the most hopeless and even depraved sinners into the kingdom of God, causing them to be born of the Spirit of God, changing them from a Jacob into an Israel, and finally bringing them to the glory of God. It is a journey from dust to glory! Only the Mighty One of Jacob could accomplish such a work. To know Him as our Savior and our Redeemer, and to experience to the full His salvation and His redemption, is the only way to face the twenty-first century with peace and hope.

All of this is highlighted by the words spoken to Jacob by God through Isaiah:

> For I the Lord thy God will hold thy right hand, saying unto thee, Fear not; I will help thee. Fear not, thou worm Jacob, and ye men of Israel; I will help thee, saith the Lord, and thy redeemer, the Holy One of Israel. Behold, I will make thee a new, sharp threshing instrument having teeth: thou shalt thresh the mountains, and beat them small, and shalt make the hills as chaff.
>
> (Isa. 41:13–15 KJV)

No words could express the tender love of the Savior more than those which He used here: "For I, the LORD thy God, will hold thy right hand." Normally it is someone who is weak, young, or infirm whose hand needs to be held. It can also be a willful and precocious child whose hand has to be held, lest they injure themselves or, even worse, destroy themselves. It is a picture of parental love and grace! In a word, it is the story of Jacob. It was the Mighty One of Jacob who held Jacob's right hand throughout his life, who tenderly but firmly brought him first to Jabbok and then to glory. "Fear not . . . I will help thee," the Lord said. Those words lie at the root of Jacob's final triumph. It will also be true of us. We have nothing to fear if the Mighty One of Jacob, our Savior and Redeemer, promises to help us.

There is no need to point out the enormous difference between "the Mighty One of Jacob" on the one hand and "thou worm Jacob" on the other. One is Almighty, and the other is weak and easily crushed and destroyed; one lives in light, and the other in darkness; one is eternal, and the other one belongs to dust! We might well ask what possible connection or interest has the Almighty God with a worm other than the fact that He created it, and it has a function to perform in its own small world!

When, however, the full meaning of the remarkable promise the Lord makes to Jacob begins to dawn on us, we are left speechless!

> Fear not, thou worm Jacob . . . Behold I will make thee a new sharp threshing instrument having teeth: thou shalt thresh the mountains, and beat them small . . .

There could be nothing more different than a worm and a threshing instrument! Can anything more powerfully illustrate the love and grace of God? He changes a worm into a sharp, new threshing instrument, and a Jacob into an Israel! The Almighty has this kind of power. It is the power of the master craftsman, the master builder, the master surgeon. It is the sensitive but nonetheless huge power to save, to redeem, and to transform a human being. For this reason, the Lord calls Himself "the Mighty One of Jacob." This Mighty One who completed the work in Jacob, will also finish the work He has begun in us.

In the forty-sixth psalm the psalmist describes a scene of earthquake and change, of war and conflict, of raging nations, and of desolation in the earth. He begins the psalm with the statement,

> God is our refuge and strength, a very present help in trouble. Therefore will we not fear . . .

It is a simple statement of God-given faith, made in conditions which would normally cause much fear. The psalmist, however, is not focused on those conditions. Instead, he declares the sovereign authority and power of God; neither the Lord nor His work and purpose will be frustrated, or even paralyzed. Through all the conflict and battle, within and without, He will achieve His goal. He will protect and sustain His own until the battle is won. For this reason, the psalmist commands us to "be still, and know that [He] is God" (vv. 4, 5, 10).

Twice the psalmist proclaims that "the Lord of hosts is with us; the God of Jacob is our refuge." He employs a meaningful term when he declares that the Lord of hosts is with us; "the Commander of the heavenly armies" is with us! Once more we are confronted with the Mighty One of Jacob! In the war and conflict over the fulfillment of God's eternal purpose, we are called to be good soldiers of Christ in the army of God. There is, however, for most of us, an even more meaningful phrase employed by the psalmist: "the God of Jacob is our refuge." When we know ourselves as "Jacobs," as failing and weak as worms, this declaration fills us with encouragement, strength, and comfort. The Mighty One of Jacob, the Commander of the heavenly armies, is with us; and the God of Jacob, the God of all grace, is our refuge. We have no reason to fear!

Dear reader, we have come to the end of these pages. The Lord must bring you and me to the same place to which He brought Jacob. If at the end we are worshipers in spirit and in truth; if we have become princes of God, and a means of blessing to others; if we have become overcomers through Him; if we reach the glory of God, it will be due only to the exhaustless love of God and His fathomless grace. It will be worth the pain of Jabbok, worth the taking up of the cross and following Him, however great the cost. Jacob's testimony will also be our testimony. The God of faithfulness, the God of all grace, the God of Jacob did not fail us!

Let the words of another lover and worshiper of the Lord Jesus, Amy Carmichael of Dohnavur, challenge you. She had her own real experience of Calvary, her own "Jabbok." When she was most needed in the work, an accident left her physically disabled for the rest of her years. Until she went to the Lord, she never walked again. Out of that disability flowed a rich and deep ministry of comfort and help to the whole world, and especially to those children of God who suffer inexplicably. Her ministry to them has been unparalleled. This is the challenging poem she wrote, which she entitled "No Scar?"

> Hast thou no scar?
> No hidden scar on foot, or side, or hand?
> I hear thee sung as mighty in the land;
> I hear them hail thy bright, ascendant star.
> Hast thou no scar?
>
> Hast thou no wound?
> Yet I was wounded by the archers; spent,
> Leaned Me against a tree to die; and rent
> By ravening beasts they compassed Me, I swooned.
> Hast *thou* no scar?

No wound? No scar?
Yet, as the Master shall the servant be,
And piercèd are the feet that follow Me.
But thine are whole; can he have followed far
Who has no wound or scar?

About the Author

Lance Lambert is one of the most distinguished Bible scholars and speakers in Israel today and has an itinerant teaching ministry worldwide. Born in 1931 he grew up in Richmond, Surrey, in England and came to know the Lord at twelve years of age. He entered the school of African and Oriental studies at London University to prepare for work in China. He studied Classical Chinese, Mandarin, Oriental Philosophy and Far Eastern History, but the revolution closed the door to European missionaries and his entry to China. In the early 1950s he served in the Royal Air Force in Egypt and later founded Halford House Christian Fellowship in Richmond. Having discovered his Jewish ancestry, Lance became an Israeli citizen in 1980 and now has a home next to the Old City of Jerusalem. His father and many members of his family died in the Holocaust.

Lance is noted for his ecclesiological views, which place him in the tradition of Watchman Nee and T. Austin-Sparks. He produces a widely appreciated quarterly audio recording called the *Middle East Update*, which gives his unique perspective on current events in the Middle East, in the light of God's Word. He has also written numerous books including *The Uniqueness of Israel*, and is presenter of the video production *Jerusalem, the Covenant City*.

Sovereign World Ltd
&
Ellel Ministries International

In a stroke of divine master planning both Sovereign World and Ellel Ministries were independently founded in the same year – 1986.

Sovereign World, founded by Chris Mungeam, has become a widely respected Christian publishing imprint and Ellel Ministries, founded by Peter Horrobin, has developed a world-wide network of Centres, each designed to resource and equip the Church through healing retreats, courses and training schools.

Twenty years later, in April 2006, Ellel Ministries purchased Sovereign World Ltd to continue the precious work of publishing outstanding Christian teaching, as well as to create a publishing arm for Ellel Ministries. It was a divine knitting together of these two organizations both of which share the vision to proclaim the Kingdom of God by preaching the good news, healing the broken-hearted and setting the captives free.

If you would like to know more about Ellel Ministries their UK contact information is:

International Headquarters
Ellel Grange
Ellel
Lancaster
LA2 0HN
UK

Tel: +44 (0)1524 751651
Fax: +44 (0)1524 751738
Email: info@grange.ellel.org.uk

For details of other Centres please refer to the website at:
www.ellelministries.org

We hope you enjoyed reading this Sovereign World book.
For more details of other Sovereign books and
new releases see our website:

www.sovereignworld.com

If you would like to help us send a copy of this book
and many other titles to needy pastors in developing
countries, please write for further information
or send your gift to:

Sovereign World Trust
PO Box 777
Tonbridge, Kent TN11 0ZS
United Kingdom

You can also visit **www.sovereignworldtrust.com**.
The Trust is a registered charity.